The Classic Trams

30 YEARS OF TRAMCAR DESIGN 1920-1950

The Classic Trams

30 YEARS OF TRAMCAR DESIGN 1920-1950

Peter Waller

IAN ALLAN *Publishing*

Contents

First published 1993

ISBN 0 7110 2160 0

Published by Ian Allan Ltd,
Shepperton, Surrey; and printed
by Ian Allan Printing Ltd at their
works at Coombelands in
Runnymede, England.

Half title page:
**Leeds 'Horsfield' No 236 awaits
departure from Beeston on 30 July
1949 with a service to Harehills. The
tram is seen is seen in the dark blue
livery of the period with the Gill
Sans fleet numbers of the style
adopted in late 1948.** *All uncredited
photographs were taken by Michael
H. Waller*

Title page:
**Royal Oak was one of the main
intersections on the Blackpool tram
system. 'Standard' No 51 is seen at
the junction with a tram for Talbot
Square via Marton.**

Introduction

At the height of tramways of the British Isles in the 1920s there were some 14,000 tramcars operational in Britain and Ireland, and they could be seen from Cruden Bay and Aberdeen in the north, to Lowestoft and Great Yarmouth in the east, to Plymouth and Camborne in the south and to Dublin and Belfast in the west. Virtually no self-respecting town or city was to be seen without its tramway system and a whole industry grew up to manufacture and maintain the varied fleets.

This book does not attempt to describe the history of the British tramcar — others have achieved this much better, most notably R. J. S. Wiseman's *Classic Tramcars*, which was published in 1986 — but rather it examines in detail a dozen or so of the most enduring designs from the period from 1920 to 1950, trams which by their history or by the interest shown in them have earned their place in the annals of transport history. The selection of types is very much a personal one; no doubt there are those who would argue for the inclusion of other types or who would query the selection of, for example, the Glasgow 'Cunarders' as opposed to the earlier 'Coronations'. I have tried to be objective in my selection; the 'Cunarders' merit their place as the single largest order of tramcars placed after

World War 2, the Blackpool 'Standards' because they represented the last 'traditional' tramcars in service, the 'Felthams' because of their dual role in the modernisation (albeit still-born) of the London company-owned network and in the final years of the system in Leeds, and so on.

The period and vehicles described represent an important phase in British transport history. More than half of the tramway systems in Britain had disappeared by the outbreak of World War 2 and had never experienced the operation of second-generation tramcars. It is doubtful whether the tram could have survived in many towns and cities even with greater investment in the 1920s given that contemporary fashion was rejecting tramways as a form of transport. But there were enough operators convinced of the tramcar's potential to see the new designs emerge; designs which were, through the adoption of streamlining and other new developments, typical of their era. Traditional methods of construction were gradually being replaced — although these developments were not wholly successful — and it is interesting to speculate as to the future of the tram in the British Isles if World War 2 had not had such a devastating effect. These, then, are the stories of some of Britain's classic trams.

Acknowledgments

I am very grateful for the assistance of many people for the completion of this book. In particular I would like to thank Alan Brotchie, W. J. Haynes, Reg Ludgate, Maurice O'Connor and David Packer for help on the photographic side. All uncredited photographs were taken by my father, Michael H. Waller. I am also grateful to Alan Brotchie for his kind permission to cite material from his article on the Dundee 'Lochee' cars published in the September 1966 issue of *Scottish Tramlines* and to Reg Ludgate for providing me with much help on the story of the 'McCreary' cars and making many useful comments. My thanks are also due to Roy Brook for permission to use material from his books on Huddersfield trams and trolleybuses. As with my earlier *British and Irish Tramway Systems since 1945* a considerable amount of information has been gleaned from the various fleet histories compiled by the PSV Circle and I am very grateful for their continued permission to cite this material where necessary. I am also grateful to John Price for reading through the book and for making useful comments thereon. Every effort has been made to ensure that the book is as accurate as possible. Any errors are the author's own.

Peter Waller
Ashford
Spring 1993

Abbreviations

BTH	British Thomson-Houston Ltd
EE	The English Electric Co Ltd
EMB	The Electro-Mechanical Brake Co Ltd
GEC	General Electric (UK Co) Ltd
HN	Hurst Nelson
LCC	London County Council
LPTB	London Passenger Transport Board
LRTL	Light Railway Transport League
LUT	London United Tramways
MET	Metropolitan Electric Tramways
M&G	Mountain & Gibson Ltd
OMO	One Man Operated
UCC	Union Construction Co Ltd
UEC	United Electric Car Co

Above left:
Belfast 'McCreary' car No 436 was one of 20 of the type built by English Electric. *W. J. Haynes*

Left:
Leeds 'Pilcher' No 281 (ex-Manchester No 104) is seen at the south end of Briggate on 23 October 1948. Nos 281 and 286 were to be the last of the type to survive in Yorkshire and were scrapped in May 1954.

1.
The Blackpool 'Standards'

The seaside resort of Blackpool was the first town to possess an electric tramway in Britain when, in 1885, Michael Holroyd Smith opened his conduit tramway along the promenade. From this start, a network of routes grew up serving both the seashore — including the route to Fleetwood — and the various town services. As a result of the varied origins of the tramway network, the corporation possessed a fleet of some 129 trams of 11 distinct types by the early 1920s. Many of these cars were increasingly aged and required replacement, whilst the sheer variety of design also caused problems. The result was the emergence of the classic 'Standard' type, a type which, four decades later, would become the last traditional British double-deck trams in regular service.

The story of the Blackpool 'Standards' is complex as the development of the type included cars rebuilt from earlier models, nominal rebuilds of older cars and wholly new vehicles. Chronologically, the first of the type were rebuilds.

The first cars to be treated were from the batch of 15 trams, Nos 27-41, that had been supplied in 1901 for the Marton route by the Midland Railway Carriage & Wagon Co. Known as 'Marton Box Cars', these four-wheel cars were fitted with Midland trucks. A number of the type had their trucks replaced by Mountain & Gibson 8ft 6in radial trucks in 1906 and 1907 (Nos 27, 28, 30, 31, 36, 40 and 41), another two (Nos 29 and 33) received Hurst Nelson 21EM 8ft 6in trucks in 1911 whilst Nos 32, 37-39 received Brush 21E trucks in the same year. UEC Preston trucks were fitted to Nos 34 and 35 in 1911. Of the 15 cars, 12 had received top covers between 1910 and 1914. In terms of the development of the 'Standard' type five trams are significant — Nos 27, 29-32.

These five trams were lengthened and rebuilt as bogie trams fitted with McGuire bogies between 1918 and 1923. Of the five, three were top covered from this stage, whilst the remaining two, Nos 30 and 31, were top-covered in 1928. In their modified form the cars were to outlive the rest of the batch by several years. The first 'Marton Box Cars' to be withdrawn were Nos 33 and 34 in the early 1920s, and the remaining unmodified cars were all taken out of service by 1927. No 31, however, was not to survive long as a top-covered tram. It became the first of the five rebuilds to be withdrawn when it was converted for use by the Engineering Department in 1934. This conversion saw the car revert to an open-top layout so that an overhead inspection tower could be accommodated. Numbered 4 in the works fleet, No 31 was to survive for almost 50 years in this guise before withdrawal in 1982 and eventual preservation at Beamish in 1984. The car has now been restored to pre-1914 condition. The remaining four cars were rendered surplus by the conversion of the Layton route to bus operation in 1936 and the arrival of the new streamlined trams. All four were withdrawn in 1937 and 1938 and were scrapped by the Corporation by December 1938.

Before the next stage of the 'Standard' programme could take place the Corporation, under the direction of its then General Manager Charles Furness, undertook considerable investment in the development of new workshops at Rigby Road. This work, which included the installation of a traverser and the building of a body shop, was to enable the Corporation to undertake the rebuilding and construction of trams (and buses). This work was completed by 1922 and the stage was, therefore, set for the next phase in the history of the 'Standards'.

In 1902 the Corporation had acquired a batch of 12 open-top cars, Nos 42-53, from the Motherwell-based manufacturer Hurst Nelson. These cars, which introduced the 'Tudor Arch' lower saloon windows that were to be a mark of the 'Standards', were top-covered between 1911 and 1914 with covers supplied by UEC and by Hurst Nelson. Wartime exigencies had led to the cars being temporarily withdrawn during 1915 and, by the early 1920s, the cars needed replacement.

After the completion of the rebuilding work on the 'Marton Boxes', the next car to be treated was 'Motherwell' No 43. Although nominally (and for accounting purposes) a straight rebuild of the earlier car, No 43 (which was to become the prototype of the 'Standard' class) received only the top cover, bogies and electrical equipment from the earlier car. Two other 'Motherwells' were to receive similar treatment in 1922/23 (Nos 46 and 53). Thereafter, the programme became subsumed into the overall 'Standard' scheme.

Of the rest of the 'Motherwell' cars five donated their top covers to 'new' 'Standard' cars bearing the same number: Nos 42 and 49 in 1926; Nos 45 and 48 in 1928; and, No 51 in 1929. One was withdrawn and replaced by a wholly new 'Standard': No 47 in 1928. No 44 was withdrawn in 1927 and not directly

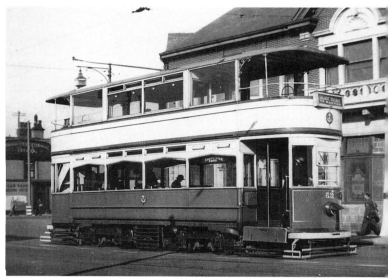

Above right:
'Standard' No 53 was one of the first three of the type to be built and dated originally from 1922-23. Like a number of the early 'Standard' cars, its history is not clearly documented, but it would seem to have inherited the top-deck, electrical equipment and bogies from the original 'Motherwell' car of the same number. Preston McGuire-type bogies replaced the original ones in February 1928 (the car later received similar bogies from No 32 as a result of a float maintenance policy) and lower-deck vestibules were fitted in August 1931. Never fully enclosed, No 53 was withdrawn in 1951 and scrapped the following year. It is seen here at Royal Oak on 29 September 1940 showing clearly the wartime white-painted buffers and shaded headlight.
Maurice O'Connor

Below right:
'Standard' No 149 was one of seven built by Hurst Nelson — four in 1924 (Nos 146-49) and three in 1925 (Nos 150-52). Originally fitted with open balconies and vestibules, No 147 received enclosed lower-deck vestibules in June 1933 (one of the last so treated) and enclosed balconies in May 1940. Withdrawn in 1966, the car is now preserved in the United States and is the only Hurst Nelson-built car to survive. It is caught at Talbot Square on 24 June 1943 again in wartime livery. *Maurice O'Connor*

No 51 was the penultimate of the 'Standards' to be built. It appeared in 1929 and is seen here in Gynn Square in 1931. As with a number of the 'Standards' No 51 was built using the top-deck of the earlier 'Motherwell' car that it nominally replaced. No 51 was built with an enclosed lower-deck from new, but was never to be fully enclosed. It was withdrawn in 1951 and scrapped in June 1954 at Blundell Street.
Author's Collection

replaced. No 50 was replaced by a new 'Standard' in 1928; the new tram probably inherited the flat top-cover from the already withdrawn No 47. This left only one 'Motherwell' in service after the withdrawal of No 51 in 1929 — No 52. This car was destined to soldier on for a further three years until its demise in December 1932. By that date, construction of 'Standards' had ceased and the car was not directly replaced.

The third group of earlier cars to be involved in the 'Standard' programme were Nos 62-8, which dated from 1911. Nos 62-64 were 'De Luxe' four wheelers manufactured by UEC in 1911. Originally fitted with Preston flexible-axle trucks and BTH GE54 controllers, the trio were converted to bogie cars — with Preston McGuire-type bogies and B510 controllers — in 1924-26. Also produced by UEC in 1911, Nos 65-68 were 'De Luxe' bogies and were fitted with McGuire-type bogies from new. Three of the four cars, Nos 65-67, were modified from 1926-33 with new B510 controllers. Although non-standard in many ways, the cars had many of the features of the 'Standard' type — in particular the top covers (with two new central large windows) were typical of those fitted to the 'Standards'. All seven cars were to be withdrawn between 1936 and 1938.

The exact train of events in 1922 is uncertain. However, the development of the 'Standard' design would seem to have been contemporaneous with the 'rebuilding' of No 43. It seems probable that the designs were completed by the end of the year and work was soon in hand on the construction of the new trams. The first four were built in 1923. These were Nos 33 and 34 (replacing the now withdrawn 'Marton Boxes') and Nos 99 and 100. These cars were fitted with the old-style Hurst Nelson-type bogies similar to those supplied in 1902. All subsequent 'Standards', however, were to be fitted with McGuire-type Preston bogies.

Hurst Nelson, whose earlier 'Tudor Arch' design for the 'Motherwells' had played an important role in the design of the 'Standards', was also to play a more significant role in the programme. In July 1923 the Transport Department was authorised to place an order with the company for four cars. These were destined to

No 99 was one of the first four production 'Standard' cars to appear and entered service in 1923. These four cars were fitted with old fashioned Hurst Nelson-type trucks (of a type new in 1902). The lower-deck platforms on No 99 were enclosed in September 1931. The car was to survive until 1954 and was scrapped in December that year at Blundell Street depot. *W. J. Haynes*

become Nos 146-149 and were delivered in 1924. This was followed in January 1925 by an order for a further three cars (Nos 150-152) which were delivered in the same year. The remaining 'Standards' were all manufactured at Rigby Road.

Between 1924 and 1929 the Corporation was to construct almost 30 'Standards'. Whilst the last of the programme was officially No 51, which emerged in February 1929, there remained enough parts for the construction of one last car. This was No 177, which entered service in July of the same year.

The 'Standards' were 33ft 10in long and could accommodate 46 passengers on the upper deck and 32 on the lower. Apart from Nos 51 and 177, all the 'Standards' were originally constructed with open lower deck vestibules, whilst all had open balconies. Three types of motor were originally adopted. The majority of the cars were fitted with BTH B265C motors. However, BTH GE54 motors were used under Nos 30-34 and 43, whilst BTH GE200 motors were fitted to Nos 27 and 29. The BTH-motored vehicles were fitted with BTH510 con-

trollers, whilst the GE54-motored cars had BTH B18 controllers. Eventually all the 'Standards' were operated with B265C motors rated at 35hp each.

Although only the last two, Nos 51 and 177, were delivered with platform vestibules, the remainder of the type were dealt with between 1929 and 1935. The first to undergo the treatment was No 153 in January 1929 and the last was No 45 in March 1935. A number of cars (Nos 38, 39, 41, 100, 155, 158 and 159) received enclosed balconies simultaneously with the enclosing of the vestibules. A further 10 cars were to be fully enclosed between 1932 and 1940. These were Nos 42, 48-50, 143, 147, 149, 150, 160 and 177. Of these 10, four were modified during 1940, with No 149 (completed in August of that year) being the last car so treated. The other cars were to remain as open balconies for the rest of their operating life.

With the appointment of Walter Luff as the new General Manager in 1933 the scene was set for one of the most radical transformations in Britain's tramway history. Whilst elsewhere in Lancashire the tram was on the retreat — and indeed was not secure in Blackpool — Walter Luff, in conjunction with English Electric, developed his stylish streamlined railcoaches and 'Luxury Dreadnoughts'. Between 1933 and 1939 more than 100 modern trams were constructed and these, combined with the closure of the Central Drive and Layton routes in 1936,

Above:
A contrast in 'Standards' is seen at Talbot Square on 9 September 1948. On the left No 177 — the last 'Standard' to be completed in July 1929 — and on the right No 28. The latter was completed in 1927 and gained enclosed lower-deck vestibules in 1930; the former was completed with lower-deck vestibules from new and gained upper-deck enclosed vestibules in June 1940. It is interesting to note that both trams retain the white-painted underframes from the wartime blackout period three years after the cessation of hostilities. No 28 was withdrawn in 1956 and No 177 the following year; both were scrapped at Thornton Gate in April 1958.

Right:
After withdrawal in 1934 'Marton Box' No 31 was converted for use as an engineering car (No 4). This conversion saw the car revert to open-top condition and gain an overhead inspection platform. It was to remain with the engineering fleet until final withdrawal in March 1982. Subsequently preserved by the North of England Open Air Museum at Beamish, the car has now been fully restored. It is seen here at Thornton Gate on 18 April 1949.

Right:
The late 1940s and early 1950s was the last period when substantial numbers of 'Standards' remained in service. On 9 September 1948 at Talbot Square No 155, built in 1926, is seen nearest the camera. It gained enclosed lower and upper-deck vestibules in August 1930. No 145, built in 1925, gained its lower-deck vestibules in January 1935 but was never destined to be fully enclosed. No 155 was to survive until 1954 and was scrapped at Blundell Street in November of that year. No 145 was to last until 1956 and was eventually scrapped at Thornton Gate in April 1958.

No 16 in December 1949 during the latter car's conversion to VAMBAC control. The experiment was unsuccessful and the car was withdrawn in 1950.

The next large inroads into the 'Standard' fleet came with the introduction of the new Roberts-built 'Coronation' cars of 1952. A total of seven cars (Nos 99, 100/44/51-3/5) were withdrawn during 1954, to be followed by a further five (Nos 28, 42, 143/5/77) between then and 1957. This left eight (Nos 40/1/8/9, 147/58-60) still in service. Of those withdrawn during the mid-1950s, the majority went for scrap — often after some length of time in store — although No 144 went for preservation to the Seashore Trolley Museum in the United States in 1955 — the first 'Standard' to be preserved. No 143 was to survive; following withdrawal in 1957, the tram was rebuilt as Engineering Car No 3 in July 1958. The work involved the removal of the centre section of the top deck, to allow for a tower, the fitting of two trolley poles — one at either end — and the installation of a Leyland 8.6 litre diesel engine. This car was renumbered 753 in 1972 and remained in service until recent fire damage — the last of a long line. It has now been replaced by a new works car.

During early 1959 two of the remaining 'Standards', Nos 158 and 159, were modified to act as illuminated cars, which resulted in No 40 being licensed for the full year for the first time since 1954. The next casualty was No 41 which split the points at Rigby Road in 1959 and was not repaired. The car was scrapped in March 1961 at Marton depot.

Although the Blackpool system was not fated to go the way of all other English electric tramways, the system did experience severe contraction during the early 1960s as the network was cut back to the Promenade route only. On 29 October 1961 the Station Road/Lytham Road route was converted to bus operation, to be followed on 28 October 1962 by the Marton route and, finally, on 27 October 1963 by the North Station/Dickson Road route. These closures, which, to contemporaries, seemed to foreshadow the final demise of Blackpool's trams, were to see the withdrawal of many cars and it was inevitable that the increasingly aged 'Standards' were amongst those to succumb eventually.

In 1961 'Standards' had reappeared on the Squires Gate route to mark the closure and this was repeated the following year for the Marton service. No 48 was the last car to operate from Royal Oak on 28 October 1962 and No 40 was the last service car from Talbot Square to Marton depot. Illuminated cars Nos 158 and 159

Following withdrawal in 1957, No 143 was converted into works car No 3 in July 1958. The work included the fitting of an overhead inspection platform and an auxiliary 8.6 litre diesel engine from a Leyland TD5. *Ian Allan Library*

allowed for the gradual withdrawal of many of the older cars. No 152 was the last car to operate to Layton on 19 October 1936.

In 1945 some 37 of the 'Standards' remained in service. There had been a number of casualties during the war. No 46 was withdrawn in 1940 and was scrapped during September of that year. Its motors and trucks were transferred to No 51 in January 1941 during maintenance and certain other parts were used to repair accident damage to other 'Standards' during 1940. No 50 had been blown over on 6 December 1940 and had not been repaired. The car had been scrapped in January 1941. In February 1945 No 38 lost its bogies to No 149; No 38 was not to operate again, although it survived in store until scrapping in October 1951.

The late 1940s were, however, to see considerable inroads made into the remaining fleet. Between 1945 and 1951 17 of the cars were withdrawn (35-7/9, 43/5/7, 51/3, 142/6/8-50/4/6/7). All of these cars were scrapped by December 1954. Of these, No 39 was significant in that it had been experimentally fitted with English Electric bogies recovered from

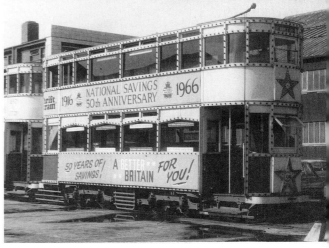

In 1959 two of the remaining 'Standards', Nos 158 and 159, were fitted with permanent illuminations. They ran in this condition until final withdrawal in 1966. The two are seen after withdrawal and awaiting their final fate. No 158 was to pass the Tramway Museum Society in May 1967 as a source of spares — it was eventually dismantled in 1978 — whilst No 159 was acquired by the East Anglian Transport Museum in April 1967, where it remains in use. *Ian Allan Library*

then followed with the official party. Three of the remaining 'Standards' were withdrawn in 1962. Nos 40 and 49 passed to the Tramway Museum Society and were transferred to the embryonic National Tramway Museum at Crich in October 1963 and December 1962 respectively. The third, No 48, was eventually sold to the Oregon Electric Railway Historical Society in the United States. It sailed from Hull in August 1964 on board the *Sibonga*, and reached Portland on 25 September of the same year.

This left only four 'Standards' in service — Nos 147/58-60 — and it was, in theory, only a matter of time before the final withdrawals. However, the veterans continued to defy the pundits and survived through 1963 and 1964; in the latter year Nos 158-60 were to be found in daily use during July, which was unusual as the cars were normally restricted to operating during the illuminations. In 1965 No 147 was restored to service as cover for the accident-damaged 'Balloons' Nos 245 and 259, and by the same year Nos 147 and 160 were the last Blackpool trams to operate with swivel-head trolley poles; the overhead on the Promenade route was designed for use with fixed-head poles.

All good things, however, had to come to an end, and 1966 was to be the last year that 'Standards' were to operate. The first to succumb were Nos 147 and 160, which were both withdrawn in theory at the end of June, having last operated on 11 April of that year. For No 147 withdrawal was to be temporary, as it was restored to service on 19 July, but for No 160 there was to be no reprieve. Its motors were required for Engineering Car No 3, and on 29 June 1966 work started on removing the required spares. The car was finally scrapped in April 1967 in Blundell Street depot. The final 'Standard' workings occurred on 29 October 1966 when Nos 147 and 159 operated an enthusiasts' tour.

On withdrawal No 147 was sold to the Columbia Park Museum in Ohio for preservation. It departed for its new home in the United States on 9 September 1967 on board the *Manchester Commerce*, reaching the New

World on 21 September. No 159 was sold to the emerging museum at Carlton Colville and departed Blackpool on 17 April 1967. The third of the surviving cars, No 158, was sold to the Tramway Museum Society as a source of spares and left for Crich on 5 May 1967. It was finally dismantled in 1978.

Thus the story of the traditional British double-deck tram came to an end. Fortunately, no fewer than six of these popular cars survive in preservation — three in Britain and three in North America — and it was appropriate that one, No 40, was to return to Blackpool in 1985 having been fully restored as one of the exhibits for the centenary of electric tramcar operation on the Lancashire Coast.

Works car No 3 was renumbered 753 in 1972. It is seen in Rigby Road depot on 30 September 1981 looking rather the worse for wear and having lost the remains of its top-deck vestibules. No 753 remains with Blackpool Transport and there are plans for the possible restoration of the car to supplement the historic cars that Blackpool has operated successfully for a decade. *G. B. Wise*

No	New	Bogies	Enclosed vestibules	Enclosed Balconies	Wdn	Fate
28	October 1927	Preston	June 1930	-	1956	Scr April 1958
33	1923	HN	August 1930	-	1940	Scr July 1940
34	1923	HN	January 1931	-	1947	Scr October 1951
35	October 1927	Preston	March 1932	-	1951	Scr December 1953
36	1925	Preston	April 1931	-	1951	Scr June 1954
37	October 1927	Preston	October 1931	-	1951	Scr December 1953
38	November 1926	Preston	June 1930	June 1930	1945	Scr October 1951
39	July 1926	Preston	February 1930	February 1930	1950	Scr September 1951
40	February 1926	Preston	December 1931	-	1962	Preserved
41	1925	Preston	May 1932	May 1932	1960	Scr March 1961
42	May 1926	Preston	February 1930	July 1938	1957	Scr April 1958
43	1923	HN*	June 1933	-	1951	Scr February 1954
45	1928	Preston	March 1935	-	1951	Scr December 1954
46	1923	HN*	November 1931	-	1940	Scr September 1940
47	February 1928	Preston	March 1932	-	1947	Scr October 1951
48	February 1928	Preston	September 1931	February 1938	1962	Preserved
49	October 1926	Preston	April 1932	March 1938	1962	Preserved
50	1928	Preston	December 1934	April 1938	1940	Scr January 1941
51	February 1929	Preston	-	-	1951	Scr June 1954
53	1923	HN*	August 1931	-	1951	Scr October 1952
99	1923	HN	September 1931	-	1954	Scr December 1954
100	1923	HN	February 1930	-	1954	Scr November 1954
142	1924	Preston	August 1930	-	1951	Scr August 1952
143	1924	Preston	December 1929	February 1932	1957	To Works Car No 3 July 1958/ Renumbered 753 in 1972
144	1925	Preston	February 1930	-	1954	Preserved
145	1925	Preston	February 1935	-	1956	Scr April 1958
146	1924	Preston	June 1932	-	1951	Scr August 1952
147	1924	Preston	June 1933	May 1940	1966	Preserved
148	1924	Preston	March 1931	-	1951	Scr July 1954
149	1924	Preston	June 1932	August 1940	1951	Scr October 1954
150	1925	Preston	October 1931	May 1940	1951	Scr April 1954
151	1925	Preston	November 1930	-	1954	Scr October 1954
152	1925	Preston	July 1930	-	1954	Scr April 1958
153	May 1926	Preston	January 1929	-	1954	Scr April 1958
154	June 1926	Preston	February 1930	-	1951	Scr September 1952
155	August 1926	Preston	August 1930	August 1930	1954	Scr November 1954
156	May 1927	Preston	October 1933	-	1951	Scr April 1954
157	June 1927	Preston	December 1930	-	1949	Scr October 1951
158	June 1927	Preston	June 1930	December 1930	1966	To TMS for spares; scr 1978
159	June 1927	Preston	February 1930	February 1930	1966	Preserved
160	Sept 1927	Preston	December 1929	March 1940	1966	Scr April 1967
177	July 1929	Preston	-	-	1957	Scr April 1958

Notes:
* These cars were later fitted with Preston McGuire bogies as follows: No 43 in November 1924; No 46 in December 1927; and No 53 in February 1928.
All cars were constructed by Blackpool at Rigby Road with the exception of Nos 146-52, which were constructed by Hurst Nelson.

2.
The Manchester 'Pilchers'

In September 1928 the General Manager of Manchester, Henry Mattinson, died. He was replaced by Robert Stuart Pilcher, General Manager at Edinburgh, who took up his new duties south of the border on 21 January 1929. Pilcher had been General Manager at Edinburgh since 1918 and had, therefore, overseen the conversion of the city's cable tramway network to more conventional electric traction.

Despite this background Pilcher was widely regarded on his appointment in Manchester as anti-tram and in his new position he was faced by a tramway system that was in a transitional stage. Mattinson had sought to expand the capacity of the tramcar fleet by rebuilding existing four-wheel cars to bogies as a means of easing the increasing problem of traffic congestion. Almost from the start of his appointment in Manchester, Pilcher saw the bus as the transport of the future and the gradual process of tramway conversion started with the withdrawal of the famous route No 53 in early 1930.

Despite this, and other early conversions, there was still no definite conversion policy agreed and there remained a pressing need for the modernisation of the tramcar fleet. The result was the construction of the 38 'Pullman' cars.

The origins of the batch lay in a report that Pilcher made to the Transport Committee on 21 February 1929 when he advocated ending the policy of 'rebuilding' in favour of the construction of a batch of completely new four-wheel cars. The trams were to be long wheelbase with a seating capacity of 61, capable of achieving 29mph and be fitted with air brakes.

Ironically, the first of the new cars, all of which were built in Manchester's own workshops, appeared in March 1930 at the same time as the first part of route No 53 was converted. When it first appeared No 266 sported a

subtle change of livery; a red band on the upper deck was incorporated into the normal Manchester livery. In addition, the roof was painted silver, although this was later amended to cream.

The new car was 32ft 6in long and was fitted with a Peckham P35 truck, built by Brush, with a wheelbase of 8ft 6in. The two motors, one for each axle, were Metro-Vick MV105 rated at 50hp each and BTH B510 controllers were adopted. Although Pilcher's original specification had called for air brakes, the cars were not fitted. Magnetic track brakes were included, although these were eventually removed from 19 of the batch. One of the cars, No 420, was fitted with regenerative braking as an experiment and tested in comparison with normal No 380. Whilst the regenerative braking showed energy savings of 23%, no further cars were converted and No 420 was converted back to normal. 27in diameter wheels were fitted on the trucks; advances in motor design had allowed for a gradual reduction in the size of wheels — which had been 32½in diameter on the bogie cars — and this meant that the trams had no step between platform and lower saloon.

The bodies, built in Manchester's Hyde Road Works, seated 40 on the upper deck and 22 on the lower. The transverse seating (upholstered in leather on the lower deck) earned the cars the official name of 'Pullmans' although the unofficial nickname of 'Pilchers' soon became established — despite the designer's instruction to the contrary.

The new car was inspected by the Transport Committee on 27 May 1930. It was originally intended that 40 of the cars would be built, at a cost of £1,800 each. In the event only 38 were constructed between 1930 and October 1932 when the last of the batch (No 676) entered ser-

Before Pilcher's arrival Manchester's tram fleet had been improved by the acquisition of 50 new cars in 1926 (Nos 1004-53), which had been built by English Electric, and by the construction of 110 nominal rebuilds by the Corporation itself between 1924 and 1930. No 1030 was to last in service until June 1948. No 358 entered service in March 1928 and is seen here on 11 August 1948 at Exchange station. It was to be withdrawn in December the same year. Both types were bogie cars (the 'rebuilds' replacing four-wheel cars); with the 'Pilchers' Manchester reverted to the four-wheel type. *Real Photographs/IAL; Michael H. Waller*

vice, although parts for the remaining two were acquired but never used. The whole batch was standard, with two exceptions: No 125 was fitted with roller axle bearings and No 266 was provided with electric heaters.

When new the cars were allocated to Hyde Road and Queens Road depots. Those allocated to the latter depot were used on the Rochdale Road routes — such as No 17 to Rochdale and No 18 to Heywood — until the abandonment of these routes. Route No 17 ran for the last time to Rochdale on 12 November 1932 and the latter, from Manchester to Heywood, was converted to bus operation on 1 May 1934. By the late 1930s, the 'Pilchers' were to be found on a number of services, including No 38 to Chorlton via West Point.

If war had not intervened then it is probable that the Manchester system would have disappeared by 1941. As it was the early years of the war saw both contraction of the system as certain trolleybus conversions were completed and expansion as other routes, recently abandoned, were reinstated. Inevitably the 'Pilchers' were affected by these changes.

One 'Pilcher'-operated route, No 51 (Miller Street-Oxford Road) was converted temporarily to bus operation on 23 March 1940 (trolleybuses taking over later) and this released eight of the type for other duties. Some of these were used on route No 42F from Exchange to Platt Lane (which was a part day and football service and which was converted finally to bus operation in the autumn of 1945) and on the re-extended route No 38 ([Albert Square]-West Point-Fallowfield). Most duties, except peak hour extras, on route No 38 were now 'Pilcher' operated.

Other routes to see 'Pilchers' in service at this time included the routes to Hollinwood (No 21) and Waterhead (No 20). The latter service, run jointly with Oldham, was converted to bus operation in August 1946 and the former in December the same year. In order to make the 'Pilchers' less conspicuous from the air, from 1940 onwards the cream roofs were painted grey, whilst from September 1940 the cars also lost the side routeboards and large side indicators. These were destined never to be replaced.

In June 1944 Manchester possessed a tram fleet of 373 vehicles. Of these 335 were bogie cars and the remaining 38 'Pilchers'. The latter

'Pilcher' No 263, which entered service in July 1932, was the penultimate of the type to appear. It is interesting to note, given Pilcher's increasing antipathy towards the tram, that the car carries the slogan ' Travel by tram or bus — cheap and convenient'. Also worthy of note are the various route stencils leaning against the depot wall in the foreground. No 263 was to be withdrawn in March 1948 and was one of seven of the type sold to Leeds. Becoming No 285 east of the Pennines, the car was destined to be finally withdrawn in April 1954. *Ian Allan Library*

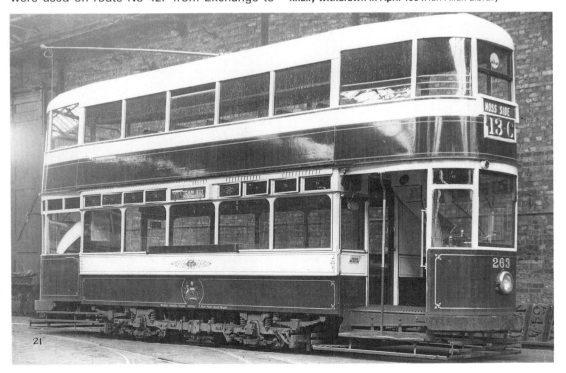

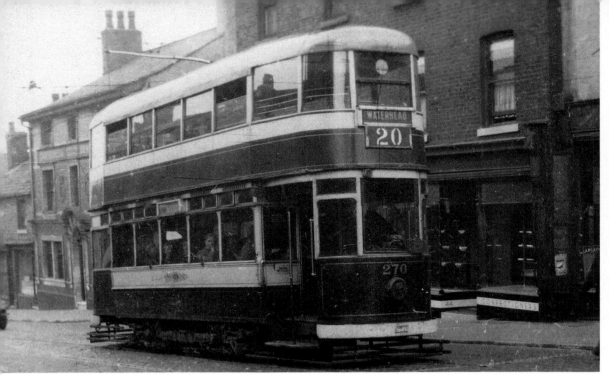

'Pilcher' No 270 is seen heading towards Waterhead on route No 20. This joint service with Oldham Corporation was finally converted to bus operation on 3 August 1946. No 270 was built originally in October 1930. Withdrawn by Manchester in May 1948, it eventually became Aberdeen No 48, being finally withdrawn in October 1955 after a career of exactly a quarter of a century. *W. J. Haynes*

cars were split between two depots: Birchfields Road had 12, whilst Hyde Road had 26. Following the conversion of route No 20 in December 1946, the cars were concentrated on Hyde Road depot and operated in particular on route No 19 (Exchange-Broomstair Bridge-Hyde) which was converted to bus operation in two stages in December 1947 and March 1948.

The Manchester abandonment policy was resumed even before the cessation of hostilities in 1945; indeed Pilcher hoped that the conversion policy would be completed by his planned retirement at the end of 1946. In the event Pilcher departed early and postwar delays meant that the abandonment programme took longer than envisaged. It was left to Pilcher's successor, A. F. Neal, to complete the conversion. On 27 July 1946 an advertisement appeared in various publications inviting bids by 22 August 1946 for 38 four-wheel trams. No 287 had already been transferred to Leeds on 18 July 1946 to enable the Yorkshire city to evaluate the type. Enquiries were received by Manchester from Aberdeen, Blackpool, Dundee and Glasgow, whilst representatives from Edin-

burgh inspected the cars on 1 August 1946. No 287 entered service in Leeds on 3 August 1946 painted in an all-grey livery. It was based at Swinegate depot, where it was to remain throughout its life in Leeds.

The remaining cars were gradually withdrawn as the Manchester system contracted. There were still the occasional high points, such as the tour of 19 October 1947, which took No 270 to Hyde, Hazel Grove and Kingsway, but the final obsequies were not long in coming. On 15 May 1948 the services from Exchange to Belle Vue/Reddish Lane were converted to bus operation and Hyde Road depot, at which all the 'Pilchers' were based, was closed as a running shed. It seems probable that this marked the final date of 'Pilcher' operation in Manchester, although the cars were not officially withdrawn until 10 June 1948. The last 'Pilcher' to leave Manchester was No 349, which departed for Edinburgh on 18 June 1948. Its departure had been delayed due to accident damage.

All the 'Pilchers' were despatched in one piece. This was unusual as it was normal practice, when moving double-deck trams by road, for the upper and lower decks to be divided.

Eventually Aberdeen acquired 14 cars at £300 each; these cars were individually selected and were widely considered to be the best of the batch. Edinburgh acquired 11 cars at £210 each (with the exception of Nos 173

Above:
Ex-Manchester No 270 is seen at Beattock heading north towards its new home in Aberdeen. The car eventually became No 48 in the granite city and was to last in service until 1955.

Below:
Edinburgh No 407, formerly Manchester No 389, heads along Waterloo Place on 25 June 1949 *en route* to Levenhall. As the 'Pilchers' were slightly longer than the rest of Edinburgh's fleet, they were limited to a number of routes and mainly operated route No 21 to Levenhall. All Edinburgh's 'Pilchers' were withdrawn in 1954.

and 676 which were slightly damaged and sold at the reduced price of £173 and £175 10s respectively), whilst the remainder went to Sunderland (seven) and Leeds (six) at £200 apiece.

Edinburgh's decision to acquire the cars was based upon a pressing need to strengthen the tramcar fleet whilst the last of the ex-cable cars was withdrawn. Numbered 401-411 in the Scottish capital, the 11 cars entered service between October 1946 and June 1948. Before entering service, the cars underwent a limited amount of modification and repainting. The modifications included the fitting of carbon skids, rather than the trolley wheel used in Manchester, as well as changes to the destination display. No 401 was mounted on a standard Edinburgh P22 truck prior to entry into service until its original P35 truck was prepared. The cars were also fitted with Maley & Taunton air brakes.

Although the 'Pilchers' were outwardly similar to the existing Edinburgh fleet — as one could have expected from Pilcher's earlier role in the development of the city's fleet — the cars were, however, 2ft 6in longer than the remainder of the fleet and were, therefore, restricted to certain routes. The cars were normally to be found operating on route No 21 from the Post Office to Levenhall, which lacked the sharp curves of certain other Edinburgh routes. One car, No 173, was tested in Edinburgh whilst still in the Manchester Corporation livery, but all were painted into the standard Edinburgh livery before entering service. No 401 was appropriately the first to appear, entering service on 1 January 1947. Three further cars, Nos 402-4, followed suit in the same year. Nos 405-7 entered service in 1948 whilst the remainder, Nos 408-11, appeared in 1949. After their entry into service, the most significant alteration was the replacement of the original P35 truck by standard Edinburgh P22 trucks salvaged from trams withdrawn.

The immediate postwar years in Edinburgh saw a continuation of the prewar policy of gradually replacing the converted cable cars with new vehicles. Although the Crewe Toll route, which had been authorised in 1934 and on which work had started in 1939, was destined not to be completed, it was not until 1950

Aberdeen No 39, which was originally Manchester No 121, is seen at Bridge of Don terminus on 24 January 1949. One of 14 of the 'Pilchers' bought by Aberdeen, the cars were destined to last until 1955-56 in Scotland. Despite hopes that one would be preserved, problems over secure storage made this impractical.

that a definite decision was made to convert the tramway system to bus operation. Initially, the plan envisaged the conversion of only a quarter of the network, but in 1952 it was announced that the entire system would be converted.

The 'Pilchers' were, therefore, destined for a relatively short life in Edinburgh. The first of the type to be withdrawn was No 404 on 26 April 1954. This was followed the next day by No 410. The rest of the remaining cars quickly followed. The last of the type, No 402, was withdrawn on 24 May 1954. The 11 cars followed the route of other recently withdrawn Edinburgh trams to the scrapyard of Connells at Coatbridge, where they were dismantled.

The 14 cars that migrated further north, to Aberdeen, were widely regarded as being the best of the type. Numbered 39-52 by Aberdeen, the cars underwent significant modifications before their entry into service. This work included modification of the destination blind display, the raising of the top deck by four inches to give more head room and to allow the fitting of bow collectors and the replacement on some cars of the existing motors by 50hp motors acquired from Liverpool. The braking arrangements were also modified. The first of the batch, No 39, entered service in February 1947, to be followed by Nos 40-42 in the same year, Nos 43-48 in 1948, Nos 49/50 in 1949 and the last two, Nos 51/52, in 1950.

As with Edinburgh, Aberdeen was considered to be one of the safest of all British tramway operators in the post-1945 era, although, again like Edinburgh, one of the proposed prewar extensions was partially built and never completed. The new acquisitions were used in Aberdeen to replace older cars, most notably a previous generation of second-hand cars — some of the ex-Nottingham cars, Nos 1-18, which had been acquired in 1936. The Aberdeen 'Pilchers' were used throughout the system, with the normal exception of the route to Woodside.

Although the Mannofield route was converted to bus operation in March 1951 to be followed by the Rosemount circle in October 1954, Aberdeen did not announce a policy of tramcar conversion until February 1955. Thereafter, the trams were destined to disappear over only three years. The first four withdrawals occurred in February 1955, when Nos 42/44/46/51 succumbed. In October 1955 a further five cars — Nos 40/41/43/48/52 — were withdrawn. These were followed in November by Nos 47 and 50, and in December by No 39. These withdrawals were the result of the conversion of the Woodside route on 26 November 1955.

This meant that only two 'Pilchers' — Nos 45 and 49 — survived into 1956. Of the two, No 45 was to be withdrawn in April 1956 and No 49 — the last 'Pilcher' to operate in Britain — was taken out of service in June 1956. The demise of the Aberdeen 'Pilchers' concentrated the minds of the now-growing tramcar preservation movement wonderfully, and the Aberdeen authorities quoted a price of £25 for one of the withdrawn cars. Whilst this may have seemed a small price to have paid, the cost, allied with the estimated £200 needed to transport the tram, proved impractical and, thus, no 'Pilcher' was to survive. Although the £225 was

Sunderland No 37 is seen at Villette Road in May 1950. This car was originally Manchester No 228. By this date the route to Villette Road had only months left before conversion; buses were to take over in November 1950. The service to Southwick lasted a year longer, being converted in September 1951. The six 'Pilchers' sold to Sunderland were to last until 1953-54 on Wearside.

promised, the problem of the lack of secure accommodation in the age before the Crich Museum remained the major stumbling block.

Whilst the failure of the preservation scheme meant that there was to be no long term survival for the type, the bodies of a number of the cars survived in Aberdeen well after withdrawal. These included Nos 45, 48 and 52, one of which was used as a staff room at King Street depot. The need to refurbish the depot as the final stages of the abandonment programme were planned meant, however, that this afterlife was destined to be relatively short. The last surviving 'Pilcher', No 49, was dismantled in November 1956.

Sunderland acquired six of the 'Pilchers' and, apart from the replacement of the trolley poles with pantographs, renovation and repainting, the vehicles remained largely in their Manchester condition. The cars were numbered 37-42 and entered service during 1947 and 1948. The first, No 37, emerged in March 1947, to be followed by No 38 in May, No 39 in August and No 40 in September. The penultimate car, No 41, entered service in January 1948. There was then a long gap before No 42 appeared in December of that year. The reason for the delay was that No 42 had been damaged in transit and was almost dismantled for spares without entering service. It was, however, repaired.

The Sunderland system was again one of the many British systems that had no definite conversion plans in 1945. Indeed, with the Durham Road extension, opened in two stages in 1948 and 1949, the system was home to one of the few postwar extensions. It was the construction of the Durham Road route, and with it the expected need for 18 additional trams, that was one of the major factors in the decision to acquire the six ex-Manchester cars. However, almost contemporaneously with the construction of the Durham Road extension, the decision was made to convert the Sunderland network to bus operation.

The conversion programme started in November 1950 when the Villette Road route was converted. Two further closures in 1951 and 1952 saw the end of the Southwick and Grangetown routes and the gradual decline of the Sunderland fleet. The first of the Sunderland 'Pilchers' to go was No 39, which was withdrawn in March 1953. This was followed in June by No 40. The other four cars remained in service until January 1954 when, on the 3rd of the month, trams were withdrawn from the Roker and Seaburn routes. The cars were dismantled by scrap merchants from Stratford-upon-Avon at Roker.

Leeds No 281 is seen at the south end of Lower Briggate *en route* to Compton Road on 24 October 1948. The tram was originally Manchester No 104 and at this time was fitted with a Peckham P35 truck. In January 1950 No 281 was, uniquely, to receive an EMB Hornless truck. At the same time its original Metro-Vick MV105 motors were replaced by two MV116s. Classified 'H1' by Leeds in 1948, the 'Pilchers' were destined for a relatively short life east of the Pennines and No 281 was scrapped in May 1954.

When first operated in Leeds 'Pilcher' No 287 retained its original number. It was, however, renumbered 280 in September 1948. It is seen here prior to renumbering *en route* to Gipton in the dark blue livery. Notice the destination display; the car retains the original Manchester arrangement of destination blind and fitting for route stencil. The latter feature would eventually be replaced by a second blind. No 280 was one of the first two 'Pilchers' to be withdrawn in Leeds, being taken out of service in late 1953. *W. J. Haynes*

The remaining six cars, which passed to Leeds as Nos 281-86, entered service between September and December 1948. They were painted in a pale blue livery with silver roof, similar to that in which No 287 (later to be renumbered 280) appeared in March the same year. The cars were also fitted with bow collectors. The cars were to be found normally operating over the Roundhay/Moortown/Lawnswood routes, but the rough riding of the cars meant that remedial action was required. Nos 285 and 286 were fitted with Skefko bearings and WT28S motors at the end of 1949. In January 1950 No 281 was fitted with an EMB hornless

truck, of 9ft wheelbase, and MV116 motors acquired from Liverpool. Later No 283 emerged in a version of the red livery, whilst Nos 281/85/86 were repainted in red and cream.

All seven cars were allocated in March and April 1950 to Swinegate. The 'Pilchers' were classified 'H1' by Leeds, but were destined to have a relatively short life in Yorkshire. The arrival of the 'Felthams' and the decision to convert the system to bus operation meant that the first two (Nos 282 and 284) were scrapped in June 1952. Nos 280 and 283 succumbed in October 1953 and the last three — the modified cars — all disappeared in April and May 1954.

Manchester 'Pilchers'

No	In service	Withdrawn	Sold to	In service	Withdrawn/ Scrapped
104	June 1931	March 1948	Leeds 281	1948	May 1954
106	June 1930	May 1948	Aberdeen 49	1948	June 1956
121	July 1930	January 1947	Aberdeen 39	1948	February 1955
125	February 1931	April 1947	Edinburgh 404	1947	May 1954
131	December 1930	March 1948	Sunderland 42	December 1948	January 1954
141	December 1930	June 1948	Aberdeen 47	1948	November 1955
144	December 1931	May 1948	Leeds 284	1948	June 1952
161	April 1931	April 1947	Aberdeen 43	1948	October 1955
163	July 1930	August 1947	Sunderland 39	August 1947	March 1953
173	September 1931	October 1946	Edinburgh 401	January 1947	April 1954
176	July 1931	December 1946	Sunderland 40	September 1947	June 1953
196	November 1931	April 1947	Edinburgh 403	1947	May 1954
217	March 1931	March 1948	Edinburgh 406	1948	April 1954
225	February 1932	June 1948	Aberdeen 50	1948	November 1955
228	November 1931	January 1947	Sunderland 37	March 1947	January 1954
231	June 1931	March 1948	Edinburgh 408	1949	May 1954
242	June 1930	April 1948	Edinburgh 409	1949	April 1954
263	July 1932	March 1948	Leeds 285	1948	April 1954
266	March 1930	May 1948	Leeds 283	1948	October 1953
270	October 1930	May 1948	Aberdeen 48	1948	October 1955
272	July 1931	April 1948	Leeds 282	1948	June 1952
274	September 1931	March 1948	Aberdeen 45	1948	April 1956
287	September 1931	July 1946	Leeds 287*	1946	October 1953
349	December 1930	June 1948	Edinburgh 411	1949	May 1954
370	May 1931	June 1948	Leeds 286	1948	April 1954
380	June 1931	June 1947	Sunderland 47	January 1948	January 1954
381	October 1930	April 1948	Edinburgh 410	1949	April 1954
389	April 1930	March 1948	Edinburgh 407	1948	May 1954
420	April 1931	April 1947	Aberdeen 41	1948	October 1955
493	February 1931	April 1948	Aberdeen 40	1948	October 1955
502	December 1930	April 1948	Aberdeen 52	1948	October 1955
503	July 1931	April 1947	Sunderland 38	May 1947	January 1954
510	February 1932	May 1948	Aberdeen 51	1948	February 1955
558	February 1932	March 1948	Edinburgh 405	1948	April 1954
610	April 1931	September 1947	Aberdeen 44	1948	February 1955
669	June 1932	May 1948	Aberdeen 46	1948	February 1955
671	May 1931	April 1947	Aberdeen 42	1948	February 1955
676	October 1932	November 1946	Edinburgh 402	1947	May 1954

* Manchester No 287 retained its original number in Leeds until it was renumbered 280 in September 1948.

3

The Leeds 'Horsfields'

Although he was to be Transport Manager of Leeds City Tramways for only three years — from August 1928 to August 1931 — R. L. Horsfield was to bequeath to the city arguably its most reliable batch of trams. These were the 104 'Showboats', which have become better known as 'Horsfields'.

When Horsfield succeeded W. Chamberlain in 1928, he inherited a large tramway system which had seen considerable modernisation over the previous decade, including the acquisition of more than 260 new trams. Indeed more than £500,000 was spent on 200 new trams in the two years before Horsfield's appointment. The bulk of these new trams were mounted on Pivotal trucks supplied by EMB. In operation these trucks were not wholly successful and future orders were to revert to conventional trucks. There still remained a need for further new cars and in 1930 the Corporation constructed four prototype cars, Nos 151-54, at Kirkstall Works.

The first to appear were Nos 151 and 152 in February 1930. No 151 entered service with a Smith Pendulum truck, although this was soon replaced by a Peckham P35. It was also fitted with two GEC WT28 motors, rated at 45hp, and GEC KA1 controllers. No 152 had a P35 truck from new, but was fitted with BTH 509 motors, again rated at 45hp, and BTH 525A controllers. The cars were the first in Leeds to be built with flush side panels. A total of 60 passengers — 23 in the lower and 37 in the upper saloons — could be accommodated in transverse two-and-one seating. The cars were 31ft 5in in length. No 153 appeared in July 1930; this car was fitted with an EMB flexible truck, from No 116A, and GEC WT28 motors. The final member of the Leeds-built quartet, No 154 entered service in September 1930. Its equipment was the same as that supplied to No 152.

With the success of the prototype cars, authorisation was given for the acquisition of 100 new cars. These were to be built by Brush and were all to be fitted with P35 trucks. Nos 155-204 were fitted with BTH type 509 motors and BTH B523C controllers, whilst the remainder received GEC WT28 motors and GEC KA1A controllers. Folding platform doors were fitted soon after delivery. All the Brush-built cars entered service during 1931, with the exception of Nos 221/50/52-4, which appeared the following year.

The cars were delivered with conventional trolley poles, but in 1935 authorisation was given to the then General Manager, Vane Morland, for the test conversion of the 'Middleton Bogies' to bow collector operation. The success of the trial led to the whole system being converted; the general change-over taking place from July 1938. The process was completed by March 1939. Although the bow collectors were patented by Jules Fischer de Tóvaros (from Budapest), the bow collectors used in Britain were manufactured under licence by the firm of Sivewright, Bacon & Co of Manchester, with the exception of those used in Glasgow. A number were also manufactured in Leeds after the war.

A further modification during the late 1930s saw a number of the cars, including No 165, receive Maley & Taunton swing link trucks; these were, however, replaced by P35s within a few years. World War 2 had little effect in Leeds (except for the increased business for the local textile trade in supplying the uniforms!), although from 1942 a number of trams, including No 223, appeared in a wartime khaki livery. Repainting in normal fleet livery did not resume until 1944.

Although the 1930s had witnessed a limited number of route abandonments, most notably

Left and below Left:
Prior to the delivery of the prototype 'Horsfields' Leeds received, between 1926 and 1928, 185 four-wheel cars built to a design of Horsfield's predecessor W. Chamberlain. Of these 35 were built by the Corporation at Kirkstall and the remainder were split equally between Brush and English Electric. The cars were fitted with EMB Pivotal trucks, which were to prove less than satisfactory in service. One of the EE-built batch, No 94, is seen at New Inn on 21 August 1949. Sister car No 92 was to be involved in a serious accident with 'Feltham' No 507 in September 1952. No 94 was one of more than 80 of these cars fitted with Peckham P35 trucks between 1944 and 1952; and in this photograph is shown with the replacement truck. Conversely, No 416 seen in July 1947 *en route* to West Park, retains, like all the Leeds-built cars, its original EMB Pivotal truck.

those sections of route (eg to Morley and Rothwell) outside the city's boundaries the period had also seen considerable investment in new infrastructure, such as the opening of the Gipton route and the immediate postwar years were to see similar developments. On the one hand certain, largely single-track sections (eg Beckett Street) were abandoned, on the other the Middleton circle was completed in two stages by mid-1949. Leeds also developed — but unfortunately never put into practice — a dramatic scheme for tramway subways in the central area. So far as the 'Horsfields' were concerned, this period saw little change except a gradual reversion to prewar standards as maintenance improved.

Under the 1948 classification introduced by V. J. Matterface, No 151 became 'C1', No 152 'C2', No 153 'C1/Flex', No 154 'C2/Peters', Nos 155-65/67-70/72-203 became 'C2/2', No 166 'C2/2/CP/AW' (sic—CP stood for Compton Parkinson and AW for Allen West), No 171 'C2/2/MV114', No 204 'C2/2/Hornless/MV114' (!) and Nos 205-54 became 'C1/2'. No 166 was reclassified 'C1/2' from 1949 whilst No 204 was reclassified 'C2/2/WT28', presumably in August 1951 when its M&T Hornless truck (which had been fitted in June 1945) was replaced by a standard Peckham P35. Although No 179 was fitted with an EMB Hornless truck (inherited

from No 396 on which it had been experimentally fitted in 1949) between July 1950 and March 1954, it does not seem to have been reclassified during that period. Likewise, the altered seating of No 203 — which saw the car accommodate 37 in the upper saloon and 27 in the lower from April 1944 until 1952 — was also not given a separate classification.

In April 1950 six of the type (Nos 249-54) were allocated, for the first time, to Torre Road depot. The rest of the class were based at Headingley (Nos 211-16), Chapeltown (Nos 201-10) and Swinegate (Nos 151-200 and 217-48). Torre Road provided cars for several routes, including those along the York Road (to Cross Gates, Halton and Temple Newsam), Chapeltown and Headingley furnished cars for routes Nos 1 (Lawnswood), 2 (Moortown via Chapeltown) and 3 (Moortown via Harehills). With the sizeable allocation also to Swinegate, the result was that 'Horsfields' were to be found over the whole of the Leeds network.

The early 1950s were to witness numerous experiments with the Leeds livery as a replacement for the earlier blue livery was sought. Inevitably a number of the 'Horsfield' cars were involved in these trials. Eventually, the red and cream livery was decided upon as standard. Other work undertaken saw the alteration of the end destination displays on a number of cars, so that the large displays were replaced by a single destination box. These were normally sited at the base of the upper vestibule window but, uniquely, No 179 had the single box placed immediately beneath the roof.

By the early 1950s the position of the tram was under threat in Leeds and, although a new pro-tram General Manager, A. B. Findlay, was appointed in late 1949 a gradual deterioration in the financial position of the Transport Department meant that the system was no longer secure. Whilst the construction of the three single-deck cars and the acquisition of the

'Felthams' from London Transport were both positive signs, the adoption of an anti-tram platform by the Labour Party in early 1953 and the party's election in May of the same year foreshadowed the end of the system. On 14 June 1953 the new Transport Committee initiated a policy of conversion and the first route to be converted — a short section of the Stanningley route had been converted earlier in the year — was the loss-making route No 14 to Stanningley on 3 October 1953, with No 166 being the last car in public service over the route. A month later, on 3 November, it was announced that the entire system would be converted to bus operation.

Initially the introduction of the 'Felthams' meant that the conversion programme heralded the end for the older cars and those earlier second-hand purchases (from Hull, Southampton and Manchester), but there was also a threat to the GEC-equipped 'Horsfields' due to problems in obtaining spares. As a result a number of the GEC-fitted cars underwent modification from late 1954 onwards. Thus Nos 214 and 253 received replacement MV 0K9B controllers, whilst another five (Nos 209/13/29/46/52) were also modified.

Two routes were converted in 1954 — No 4 to Kirkstall Abbey and No 10 to Compton Road. These conversions saw further withdrawals

Above:
Two of the production 'Horsfields' are seen at Roundhay Park on 1 August 1938. No 163 (one of the cars fitted with BTH equipment), nearest the camera, is on route No 14 to Stanningley, whilst No 244 (one of the GEC-equipped cars) is on route No 5 to Beeston. *Maurice O'Connor*

amongst the older cars, most notably the 'Pivotals' and the 'Beeston Air Brakes'. Although one route was to be converted in April 1955 (No 11 to Gipton), it was the conversion of two routes — No 8 to Elland Road and No 6 to Meanwood — that led to the first withdrawals amongst the 'Horsfields'. A total of 19 were withdrawn after these abandonments, although they were not scrapped until December at the earliest. Between December 1955 and December 1956 a total of 26 of the GEC-fitted cars were disposed of by the Transport Department at the Low Fields Road yard — these were Nos 207/08/10/11/18/20/23/25-28/30/32-34/37-39/41/43-45/48-51. Despite the problems with spare parts 14 of the GEC-fitted cars were, however, overhauled and repainted and all but one of these survived until mid-1959 — the one exception was No 205, which was withdrawn earlier in the same year. In all, 17 of the GEC cars were to survive into the final year of the system.

Two routes were to be withdrawn during 1956 — the prestigious route No 1 to Lawnswood in March and No 16 to Whingate and New Inn in July — although the year also saw the temporary reintroduction of limited services to Elland Road as a result of the Suez crisis. By September 1957, and the next versions — the reintroduced service to Elland Road being withdrawn in March 1957 — the only intact class was represented by the 50 members of the BTH-fitted 'Horsfields', but this was not to remain the case for long. The first withdrawal, of No 189, occurred following an accident on 4 November 1957. This car exchanged numbers with the later-preserved No 180 and the latter car spent its last two years as No 189. The withdrawn car was not scrapped (by Johnson of Churwell) until March 1959. Two other pairs of 'Horsfields' were to swap numbers in December 1957 — No 212 with No 242 and No 219 with No 221.

1958 was destined to be a relatively quiet year for Leeds, with no routes converted to bus operation, although No 197 was trapped in a snowdrift for a day on the Middleton route on 25-26 March! That being said, however, the process of gradual decline continued; for example, the last two cars to be repainted fully, Nos 153 and 154, emerged in July 1958. On 28 March 1959 a total of three routes were converted — Nos 3 to Moortown via Harehills, No 12 to Middleton via Moor Road and No 26 to Middleton via Belle Isle. 'Horsfields' Nos 160 and 171 were the last cars to operate in public service on the Moortown route, with No 192

Seen in City Square on 18 September 1948, No 201 is heading off towards the northern terminus of Lawnswood. Pictured here in blue livery, No 201 was one of one of 28 'Horsfields' to survive until the closure of the system in 1959 and on withdrawal was scrapped by J. W. Hinchliffe Ltd at Swingate depot.

One of the Leeds-built prototype cars, No 152, waits at the Belle Isle terminus on 24 October 1948. Built in 1930, No 152 was given the classification 'C2' under the 1948 scheme. On withdrawal it was scrapped by Johnson, of Churwell, in March 1959. Behind the car can be seen one of the stylish 'Middleton Bogies'.

being used to carry civic dignitaries. One further route, No 25 to Hunslet, was converted to bus operation on 18 April. These conversions, which included the abandonment of the city's last new stretch of route, saw the demise of many cars, including all the surviving GEC-fitted trams. The majority of cars withdrawn at this stage were sold to George Cohen and taken to a yard at Holbeck for dismantling. Cars withdrawn at this stage included Nos 151/53/54 — the last of the Leeds-built prototype cars — and 19 of the BTH-fitted trams. This left a total of some 28 'Horsfields' operational, along with the remaining 'Felthams', over the four surviving routes.

These four routes, which all ran east along the York Road to Harehills Lane (No 17), Cross Gates (No 18), Halton (No 20) and Temple Newsam (No 22), were destined to be con-

No 169, in the then new red livery, is seen outside Central station on 26 April 1951. The section of route from Half Mile Lane to Stanningley was abandoned in January 1953 — the last such conversion before wholesale abandonment of the trams in Leeds became official policy in June of the same year.

verted on 7 November. On the final day No 158 was the last service car to Halton, departing at 4.34pm, and No 181 the last to Cross Gates at 4.39pm. No 181 could also lay claim to being the last Leeds tram in public service. Appropriately all 10 cars in the closure procession were 'Horsfields' — Nos 178/72/71/98/91 to Cross Gates and Nos 173/76/89/75/60 to Temple Newsam. Of these 10, Nos 160 and 178 (which carried the official party) were illuminated. After closure, 25 of the remaining cars were sold to J. W. Hinchcliffe Ltd and were scrapped at Swinegate — the last being disposed of in February 1960. Of the remaining three, No 189 (the former No 180) passed to the Tramway

Museum Society, reaching Crich on 6 February 1960, and is now on display, fully restored, at the National Tramway Museum. Two others were also to survive. No 160 was acquired by the Leeds City Museum and stored by the museum on the Middleton Railway. Unfortunately, following vandalism, the car was broken up in 1963. A second car, No 202, also went to the Middleton Railway and, after the disposal of No 160, this car was passed to the museum. Failure to obtain secure accommodation meant that this car, also, was heavily vandalised and by the late 1960s it was in a derelict condition. It, too, has been dismantled. This leaves only No 180 to survive from this attractive class.

On 14 March 1959 'Horsfield' No 181 heads past Middleton Colliery on route No 18 to Cross Gates. By this date the only types of car in service in Leeds were the 'Horsfields' and the 'Felthams'; No 181 was one that survived until the end, being withdrawn in November 1959. After withdrawal the car was scrapped at Swinegate depot. *D. Trevor Rowe*

4

The Dundee 'Lochees'

Dundee possessed the smallest of the tramway networks in the 'Big Four' cities north of the border and the most traditional. Whilst Aberdeen, Edinburgh and Glasgow all saw fleet modernisation during the 1930s and 1940s, Dundee's last new tramcars were the batch of 10 built by Brush — the 'Lochee' cars in 1930.

In 1926 D. P. Morrison was appointed Dundee's manager. He inaugurated a period of considerable modernisation of the tramcar fleet, a programme which saw the majority of the trams rebuilt and retrucked. There remained a need for additional trams to supplement the relatively few new trams acquired since 1919. Tenders were, therefore, invited for the construction of 10 new cars. The winning tender was received from Brush — at a price of £1,320 per car — whilst unsuccessful bids for the bodies were made by Hurst Nelson, English Electric and Pickering. EMB were to supply the trucks. The order with Brush was placed in July 1929. The total cost of each car was £2,400.

The first of the batch, No 19, was delivered on 3 October 1930 in two parts. Unlike the traditional Dundee trams, the new cars were flush-sided although still conventional in terms of construction. The EMB flexible axle trucks had a wheelbase of 8ft 6in and were fitted with two Dick Kerr DK105/1C high-speed lightweight 50hp motors. Although unsuccessful in their bid to build the complete cars, English Electric did, however, supply the electrical equipment. EMB air brakes were fitted as were magnetic brakes, although the latter were removed in 1934. The cars were the first Dundee trams to be completely upholstered and seated 34 in the upper saloon and 28 in the lower. They were to remain the only Dundee trams with transverse seating in the lower saloon and upholstered seats in the upper.

Following completion, No 19 was first used in service on the Blackness-Downfield route on 17 October. It was soon followed into service by Nos 20 and 21. It seems probable that the cars were designed for the Ninewells service, since tests were undertaken along the route during November and December 1930. However, an immediate problem soon became apparent — the cars were too wide.

Until the delivery of the 'Lochee' cars, all of Dundee's trams varied in width from 5ft 6in to 6ft 7in. The new cars were, however, 7ft 1½in wide and this meant that they were too wide to

Dundee's first 10 electric trams were delivered in 1900. This batch, Nos 1-10, were built by ERTCW as open-top, open-vestibuled double-deck bogie cars. During their 55-year life, the cars underwent considerable modification — top-covers were fitted between 1907 and 1910 and the trams became fully-enclosed four-wheelers in 1930-31. No 2 is seen on Balgay Road on 10 March 1951. With the rebuilding of the older cars, Dundee achieved considerable standardisation and, in many ways, was the last traditional tramway system to close.

The last batch of trams bought by Dundee prior to the 'Lochee' cars were Nos 91-99, which were fully-enclosed double-deck four-wheelers built in the Corporation's own workshops in 1923-26. The cars were renumbered Nos 29-33 and 53-56; No 55 is seen at Maryfield on 3 June 1954. These were the last new trams to be built by the Corporation, although the Works undertook considerable rebuilding of older vehicles.

operate simultaneously over certain routes since the space between the running lines was too narrow. The minimum separation on the Ninewells route was 4ft 2in, that on the routes to Maryfield, Blackness and Downfield was only 3ft 6in. The problem was, moreover, compounded by a number of severe corners, such as that from Commercial Street to Meadowside on the Downfield route which was of only 42ft radius.

The problems with the width of the cars led to their temporary storage in Maryfield depot whilst decisions as to their future were made. It

was decided that the Lochee route would be the most suitable for the operation of the cars and work was immediately undertaken to alleviate any possible trackwork problems. The Lochee route had been rebuilt already in 1923-24, but a certain amount of work was required to make it suitable for the 'Lochee' cars. The route was, therefore, modified to a minimum separation of 4ft 4in and certain curves improved so that cars of 31ft 6in length and 7ft 3in width could safely operate. The 'Lochee' cars were allocated to the service from December 1930 and, although single cars did venture away from the route, it was to be their home for the next quarter century. The small depot at Lochee was utilised to accommodate them.

The problems with the cars were not yet over. In operation it appeared that the 50hp motors were regularly burning out. Investigation showed that the problem occurred when the trams were descending Lochee Road on the inward journey and when the driver swung the controller back from seventh notch in order to brake. The strain caused on the motors resulted in them burning out.

Although the cars were delivered with conventional trolley poles, they were not to remain so fitted for long. In early 1934 No 27 became the first Dundee car to be fitted with a Fischer bow collector, and the entire batch also received bow collectors over the next year at a price of £20 per car. As the overhead was mod-

The first of the 'Lochee' cars, No 19, entered service on the Blackness-Downfield route on 17 October 1930. On this first day No 19 picks up passengers in the High Street before departing towards Blackness. In the background, a second car can be seen heading eastwards on the Baxter Park route. This route was to be converted to bus operation on 2 October 1932. The Courier, *Dundee*

ified on other routes so the whole Dundee fleet was converted.

The cars were delivered with improved destination displays, including a route number display. The rebuilt cars were also modified to take account of this alteration. From February 1933 the Lochee route became No 23. However, largely due to the location of the route number box in relation to the curved seat in the vestibule area, the use of the route numbers on the trams was discontinued and all had the fixtures removed during 1937-38.

The new trams were widely seen in the city as being particularly luxurious — a contemporary cartoon showed the conductor as waiter serving tea to the passengers in the lower saloon — and there were rumblings of discontent about their allocation solely to the Lochee route. The standard of luxury was, however, diminished when in the summer of 1934 the electric heaters were disconnected. It was esti-

A dramatic view looking up Reform Street in c1933 with No 24 heading out-bound towards Lochee. The cars were originally delivered with trolleypoles, but from early 1934 were, along with the rest of the Dundee fleet, converted to Fischer bow collectors. The car shows route No 23, but the use of route numbers on tram routes was not long-lived and the cars lost their route number boxes during 1937-38. The Courier, *Dundee*

mated in December 1933 that this modification would save around £500 per car each year. In 1934-35 the cars also lost their magnetic track brakes. A further slight change in 1936 saw the Corporation's coat of arms modified.

To operate the Lochee service a total of eight cars were required. All 10 of the 'Lochee' cars were thus based at the small depot at Lochee for the service. The depot capacity was such that two other cars were also normally based there, giving a total allocation of 12.

As elsewhere, the onset of World War 2 led to some slight changes. The destination blinds

The High Street was the hub of Dundee's tramway system. Here, in the early 1930s, seven trams — of varying types — can be seen with No 1 *en route* to Lochee closest to the camera. The introduction of route number boxes to the Lochee cars led to a similar (again shortlived) modification on the older rebuilt cars. The Courier, *Dundee*

were removed and the paintwork modified with white-painted lifeguards, fenders, axle-box covers, etc. These modifications gradually disappeared towards the end of the war.

In 1945 the Dundee system remained much as it had before World War 2. There were some 60 trams operating over five routes radiating out from the city centre. Although suffering from lack of investment, there was to be no policy of tramcar abandonment until the mid-1950s. In the meantime, however, the existing tram fleet was to continue to soldier on. Investigations were made into the possible acquisition of new or second-hand cars, but the problem which had dogged the introduction of the 'Lochee' cars — the unusually narrow separation of the running tracks — rendered unsuitable most of the trams then being made available.

In 1949 a slight alteration was made to the 'Lochee' cars, when their original two-piece windscreens were replaced by a single pane of glass.

Dundee took a great deal of pride in its tramcar fleet and all were well maintained. Prewar standards of painting and lining out ensured that the green and white trams were always attractive. However, increasing commercial pressure and the declining financial position of the Transport Department led, in November

1950, to the introduction of external painted adverts. The adoption of these adverts led, in March 1951, to the loss of the Council's coat of arms from the front end of the top deck of the trams when the vehicles were repainted. Likewise, the lining out — which had traditionally been particularly complex — was also simplified from 1950 onwards.

The increasing age of the tram fleet, and the inability of the Council to obtain replacements, allied with the almost dominant anti-tram feeling of the 1950s led to Col McCreary, then the former General Manager of Belfast, being invited in 1952 to produce a report on the future of the system. Inevitably this report advocated the abandonment of the trams. However, little was done until the appointment of W. L. Russell as the new General Manager in 1953. In late 1954 Russell produced a confidential report which again advocated abandonment and on 6 January 1955 it was decided to withdraw experimentally the Blackness-Downfield route.

Although the system was now under threat, a start was made in early 1955 on the overhauling and repainting of the 'Lochee' cars. By the end of April, four (Nos 20-22/25) of the cars had been completed.

The temporary closure of the Blackness-Downfield route took place on 26 November 1955 and many of the older cars were quickly disposed of. The inevitable decision to convert the rest of the system was made on 5 July 1956. The end of the Dundee system was not long in coming. Trams were withdrawn from

The attractive lines of a 'Lochee' car when brand new. This illustration shows clearly the dark green and white livery and highly ornamental lining out that was such a feature of the Dundee system. *Alan Brotchie Collection*

Above:
Although normally limited to the Lochee route due to gauge problems, single 'Lochee' cars were able to venture on to the rest of the system. No 27 is seen at Downfield whilst operating an LRTL-organised special on 16 August 1950. The superb condition of the car and the lack of advertisements are worthy of note.

Below:
Latterly, as elsewhere, standards gradually deteriorated. Adorned by advertisements and looking slightly the worse for wear, No 22 is caught at Ninewells — again off its normal stamping ground — on 20 April 1954.

The scene on the High Street on 22 April 1951 with 'Lochee' car No 25 (ultimately fated to be the last car) arriving and No 10 departing towards Blackness. Although not obvious, the extra width of the 'Lochee' car is apparent by studying the centre windows at the front of both top-decks.

the final routes (Maryfield-Ninewells and Lochee) on 20 October 1956. 'Lochee' car No 25 was the last car, although the actual closure was not officially marked — a sad way to end more than 50 years of electric tramcar service in the city.

Following the closure a number of trams made their way from Lochee depot to the depot at Maryfield for scrapping. The last of these ghost movements occurred on 25 October, when No 21 made its stately progress eastwards. At closure all the remaining trams were sold to Birds of Stratford-upon-Avon for a grand total of £12,500. The deal covered the remaining 31 passenger cars, including the 10 'Lochee' cars, and works car. Prior to the sale local enthusiasts had been offered one of the 'Lochee' cars for preservation on the proviso that immediate alternative accommodation be found. When this proved impossible, the offer of the car had to be declined and thus none of Dundee's electric trams was to survive. All were to be dismantled by Birds within 10 days of closure; a sale of souvenirs and small items was held at Lochee depot on 27 October 1956.

On 28 June 1955 No 24 heads out of central Dundee *en route* for Lochee. It is seen using the crossover at the south end of Lochee Road. The tracks to the left led to the Central depot and workshops.

The town of Huddersfield, in the industrial West Riding, has one great claim to fame in public transport history — it was the location of Britain's first municipally-owned transport system. A steam tram service was established by the Corporation in 1883 on the unusual gauge of 4ft 7¾in. The choice of the gauge — just as on the much larger system in Glasgow — was based upon the operator's desire to run conventional railway wagons over the system in order to serve local industry. Experimentation had shown that, by adopting such a gauge, it was possible to run standard gauge wagons, with their different wheel profile, on grooved tram track. The Huddersfield network was progressively electrified during the early 1900s and, like many other similar systems, was largely complete by the middle of that decade. A small number of extensions were built after 1904, culminating with that to Brighouse which opened on 12 March 1923.

Although the system was not to grow significantly, there was continuing investment in vehicles through the period with both new cars acquired during the 1920s and older ones rebuilt. There was, as yet, no direct threat to the tram system and in February 1930 the Transport Committee authorised the purchase of six new, fully-enclosed, trams. The trams, to the specification of the General Manager A. A. Blackburn (who had been in the post since 1918), were ordered in May 1931 with

English Electric at Preston supplying the bodies and Maley & Taunton the trucks. The bodies were all delivered between 12 August and 8 September of that year and the trucks between 5 and 10 August.

Work proceeded rapidly on the completion of the first car and No 138 was publicly launched on a run to Outlane on 20 August 1931. The new car was 29ft 0in long and was fitted with a Maley & Taunton swing link truck of 8ft 0in wheelbase and Hoffmann roller bearings. Two English Electric 50hp motors, of DK105.5H-type, were fitted, as were DB1 K33E controllers. Seating, largely transverse, was provided for 36 on the upper deck and 20 on the lower. In a new departure, although the lower saloon retained moquette covering on

Delivered in late 1919, No 108 was one of a batch of 20 cars built by English Electric and delivered in the immediate postwar era. The car is seen on the reserved track section on the Brighouse route at Fixby. The Brighouse route was opened in 1923 and was Huddersfield's last extension. This batch of 20 cars was the last delivered to Huddersfield with open top-deck balconies; the next batch, Nos 127-36, were introduced in 1923 and were also built by English Electric.
W. J. Haynes

Above:
Huddersfield 'English Electric' car No 139 heads along John William Street on 4 August 1935 on route No 10 to Honley. Although the 'English Electric' cars were largely limited to the Marsden service by this date they did appear on other services occasionally. When sold to Sunderland in 1938, No 139 became No 35. *Maurice O'Connor*

The last of the first batch of 'English Electric' cars, No 142, is seen in the Corporation's Longroyd Bridge Depot. On withdrawal, this car became Sunderland No 32.
W. A. Camwell

the seats, the upper saloon, for the first time, had upholstered seats in red leather.

All six cars, No 137-42, were in service by 24 September 1931. They were painted in a new version of the existing Huddersfield red and cream livery, with Post Office red replacing the earlier shade. The cars also had smaller than normal fleet numbers, although standard sized numerals were applied after the first repaint. When new, two each of the type were allocated to the following three routes: Road Lea-Birkby; Bradley-Marsden; and Honley-Sheepridge.

1932 was to prove a seminal year for the Huddersfield system. Although the final two English Electric cars, Nos 143 and 144, were delivered, it was also the year that saw the first tentative steps towards the adoption of the trolleybus system that was ultimately to supplant the trams. The two new cars were largely similar to the earlier batch, although they were 1ft longer (at 30ft 0in) and were fitted with two English Electric DK105-13H motors, rated at 50hp. Seating capacity was increased to 40 in

the upper saloon, although the lower remained at 20. Later modifications saw the seating capacity of the first batch increased to 38 on the upper saloon and to 42 in the last two. All the cars were fitted with forward-facing end top seats. This was an unusual feature. The new cars were also delivered with the standard sized fleet numbers.

Much more significant for the Huddersfield system was, however, the decision taken on 5 January 1932, following reports produced by Mr Blackburn and the Borough Engineer, to convert the single-track Almondbury route — then in need of reconstruction — to trolleybus operation. The momentum towards wholesale trolleybus operation was increased when, following the retirement of Mr Blackburn in April 1933, H. C. Godsmark was appointed General Manager. Godsmark had come from Nottingham, a city rapidly converting its tramway system to trolleybus operation, and was widely regarded as being pro-trolleybus. Further progress was made towards trolleybus operation when the Almondbury route was inaugurated on 4 December 1933 and further routes followed in 1934. In April 1935 it was decided

that all the remaining tram routes would be converted to trolleybus operation.

By this time — indeed ever since the arrival of Nos 143 and 144 — the English Electric cars had been largely limited to the Bradley-Marsden route, although they were occasionally seen elsewhere and, thus, when the Marsden route was converted in April 1938 the eight cars were rendered surplus to requirements and withdrawn. This might have been the end of the story but for developments on the northeast coast. The Huddersfield system was to survive the withdrawal of its most modern cars by barely two years, becoming one of the few systems to close completely during World War 2 when the Brighouse route was converted on 29 June 1940.

Below:
The first of the Huddersfield cars, No 137, became No 33 in Sunderland in 1938. It is seen here at the Museum on 1 September 1954, barely a month before the end of the Sunderland system. Sunderland, like Huddersfield, adopted a red and cream livery, which simplified the introduction of the cars in the northeast. *Maurice O'Connor*

Above:
Sunderland No 31 heads along the Durham Road route towards Plains Farm. After the opening of the final extension of the Durham Road route in February 1949, the original terminus (of the 1948 extension) became Humbledon. The crossover at Plains Farm was largely used by peak hours short workings. No 31 was originally No 138 in the Huddersfield fleet. The car has, by this date, received a smaller background panel to the fleet numeral.
W. J. Haynes

Below:
No 36 was the last of the ex-Huddersfield cars to enter service in Sunderland and is pictured here with the slightly oversize background to the fleet number — a consequence of Sunderland's two-digit number replacing the three-digit number in Huddersfield. No 36 was originally No 143 in Huddersfield, one of the two cars delivered in 1932 which had a slightly increased seating capacity (60 rather than 56).
W. J. Haynes

During the 1930s the Sunderland system underwent considerable investment. Whilst similar sized networks in other towns and cities were contracting, Sunderland was to witness both new extensions as well as new and second-hand trams. A veritable mixture of second-hand cars were acquired — from Portsmouth, London, Accrington and Mansfield — and, following the opening of the Dykelands Road extension to Seaburn on 10 May 1937 and later improvements to service frequencies, the search was on for further acquisitions. The continuing conversion of the London system enabled Sunderland to acquire a number of ex-Ilford Corporation cars (which became Nos 2-9 in Sunderland) whilst, the conversion of the Marsden route in Huddersfield on 9 April 1938 released the eight English Electric cars.

The whole batch of eight was acquired by Sunderland at a price of £225 each, plus £75 for spares. The work undertaken on the cars in Sunderland included the regauging of the trucks to 4ft 8½in, the fitting of pantographs, the removal of route number indicators and platform doors. As the Sunderland livery was also red and cream, little was done to the exterior at this stage with the exception of adding the Sunderland fleet numbers — on a cream box above the headlamp — and coat of arms. The first to enter service was No 29 (Huddersfield No 144) and the remainder followed in sequence: Nos 30 (ex-No 141), 31 (138), 32 (142), 33 (137), 34 (140), 35 (139) and 36 (143). Although the cars were later repainted, with smaller cream panels on the dashes, they were never to receive the 'streamlined' livery adopted for much of the rest of the Sunderland fleet. Amongst services operated in prewar days was that to Seaburn via Fulwell.

As an industrial centre and port, Sunderland was a natural target for enemy action during World War 2. The Seaburn route, via Roker, was suspended on 5 December 1939 to facilitate the installation of coastal defences and the tramways were also to suffer slight damage from bombing raids; both depots — at Wheat Sheaf and Hylton Road — were hit by bombs during March 1943. Apart from minor damage, the trams were, however, to escape relatively unscathed. With the coming of peace in 1945, thoughts turned again to the development of the tramway system. Further second-hand trams were acquired — this time from South Shields, Manchester and Bury — whilst work commenced on the construction of the Durham

Sunderland No 32 is seen at Roker in May 1950. This was originally Huddersfield No 142, the last of the first batch of six slightly shorter cars. No 32 was one of four of the ex-Huddersfield cars to take part in the closure procession in Sunderland in October 1954.

Pictured at Roker in May 1950, Sunderland No 35 was originally Huddersfield No 139. This car was seriously damaged in an accident on the Durham Road reservation in October 1950 and was almost completely rebuilt at Hylton Road Works. It re-entered service in mid-1951 and was another of the quartet that featured in the closing procession.

Road extension (which was opened in two stages on 21 February 1948 and 7 February 1949).

Paradoxically, however, the decision had been made on 11 January 1947 to abandon the trams. This decision had been based on recommendations, including the go-ahead for the Durham Road extension, made at the end of 1946. The policy was, in theory, to be one for the long-term — indeed it was speculated that Sunderland's trams could still be operating in 1971! However, the pace of change was to be accelerated through the deaths of General Manager Charles Hopkins on 16 October 1948 and his successor, H. W. Snowball, on 1 January 1952. Although the first two conversions — Villette Road on 5 November 1950 and Southwick on 2 September 1951 — had already taken place, the new General Manager, appointed from 1 July 1952, Norman Morton, was a 'bus man' and it came as no surprise, when, in September 1952, it was decided to convert the whole system more rapidly.

Although the system was now under threat, car No 35, which had been seriously damaged in an accident on the Durham Road reservation in October 1950, was almost completely rebuilt at Hylton Road Works and re-entered service in mid-1951. Elsewhere, such damage could well have led to the premature withdrawal of the car.

On 30 November 1952 the Grangetown service was converted. These conversions meant that Sunderland now had a considerable surplus of trams and the first Huddersfield car to be withdrawn, No 29, succumbed in mid-1953. As with the majority of other Sunderland trams withdrawn before 1954, it was sold for scrap to a merchant at Benton (near Newcastle). The next closures occurred on 3 January 1954 (the routes to Seaburn, via Roker, and Circle) and further withdrawals reduced the Sunderland fleet to only 29 cars, including the seven surviving ex-Huddersfield examples.

The ex-Huddersfield cars were also to survive the next closure, that of the Durham Road route on 28 March 1954. This conversion meant that only one route — to Seaburn via Fulwell — remained and that was destined to be converted on 1 October 1954. Of the ex-Huddersfield cars, four — Nos 31, 32, 34 and 35 — were used in the farewell procession. Unfortunately, none of the type was destined to be preserved.

6.
The Blackpool 'Streamliners'

Although the 'Standards' were to ensure that Blackpool's tramway system was to outlast the 1920s, it was to be a major revolution that enabled the system to survive through the 1930s and beyond. Whilst other holiday resorts, such as Southport and Scarborough, were rapidly abandoning their trams, in Blackpool a beacon of modernisation was lit which ensured that the system continued to develop.

At the heart of this revolution was one man — Walter Luff — who was appointed General Manager in January 1933. He realised that without significant investment the fate of Blackpool's system was in the balance. He was faced by increasing pressure for the conversion of the 'town' routes and by stagnating passenger levels. On 20 February 1933 he presented a five-year strategy for the system. Part of this strategy involved the modernisation of the Promenade route, whilst the 'town' routes would receive only basic maintenance until their future was determined. As part of the modernisation plan, he persuaded the Council to fund the construction of a prototype streamlined car at the cost of £2,000. With remarkable speed, this prototype car, No 200, was completed within months and was unveiled in Blackpool on 19 June 1933, when, coincidentally, the Conference of the Municipal Tramways and Transport Association was taking place in the town. The speed of production was assisted by the fact that English Electric, through their Sales Manager William Lockhart Marshall, had already started to develop a modern-style tramcar with Blackpool very much in mind, even before Luff's appointment

No 200 was built by English Electric at nearby Preston, and was fitted with English Electric 4ft 0in bogies. Two English Electric Type 305A motors, rated at 57hp each, were fitted. The body was fitted with centre entrance/exit and each saloon could accommodate 24 seated passengers. There were, in addition, four folding seats on the platform, but these were subsequently removed. The car was fitted with English Electric Z4 controllers, a type which was also used on many of the subsequent deliveries. In order to emphasise the break with the past, No 200 was unveiled in a new green, rather than red, and cream livery. The prototype entered public service on 24 June and was an immediate success.

The success of the prototype car led to an order on 26 June for a further 24, Nos 201-24, at a cost of £2,356 each. These cars were delivered in 1933-34, with Nos 201 and 202 entering service on 23 December 1933 and No 203 on 6 January 1934. The production cars were two feet longer than the prototype, in order to improve leg room in the driver's cab. The only teething problem was a fault with the bogie frames, which all had to be modified by English Electric during 1935. On 1 March 1934 the new cars took over the Lytham Road route from Gynn Square to Squires Gate.

Luff now turned his attention to other elderly members of the fleet — the 'Dreadnoughts' and the 'toastracks'. On 25 September 1933 the Transport Committee authorised the acquisition of two further prototype cars from English Electric. Immediate hopes for a bulk order were dashed, however. In February 1934 the two new cars — No 225 the 'Luxury Toastrack' and No 226 the 'Luxury Dreadnought' — were delivered and the Committee authorised the acquisition of 11 more of the toastracks (or 'Boats' as they became better known), 12 further 'Dreadnoughts' and 14 fully-enclosed double deckers. The total value of the order was almost £100,000.

No 226 was fitted with English Electric 4ft 9in bogies and two English Electric Type 327A

Above:

Constructed to a patented design of a Mr Shrewsbury of Camberwell — a patent which Blackpool Corporation later acquired — the 20 'Dreadnought' cars, built between 1898 and 1902, were an attempt to cope with the massive crowds using the Promenade route. It was these cars that the Luff-designed double-deck trams were designed to replace. Fortunately, one of the 'Dreadnoughts' was to survive after withdrawal in the mid-1930s and is now displayed at Crich. It is seen in its home town on 16 July 1960 having been restored for the 75th anniversary celebrations. *Roy Marshall*

Below:

The last single-deck trams constructed prior to the launch of No 200 were the 10 'Pantograph' or 'Pullman' cars of 1928. These cars, built for the service to Fleetwood, represented the first phase in the replacement of the earlier Blackpool & Fleetwood Tramroad Co Ltd's fleet. The company's cars had been inherited by Blackpool Corporation in 1920. The new streamlined trams were to lead to the withdrawal of the remaining ex-company cars by 1939. 'Pullman' No 175 is seen at Fleetwood on 19 September 1948.

No 249 which remained at Preston for an exhibition and did not enter service until April 1935, all were in service by October 1934. The cars were largely identical to the prototype. The major difference was a slightly longer cab, which gave the cars a more definite slope than the original. Following on from the 'Luxury Dreadnoughts', the first of the all-enclosed streamlined cars, Nos 250-63, arrived in December 1934 and all were in service by April 1935. These cars, which became known as 'Balloons' seated 44 in the upper saloon and 40 in the lower. Like the earlier open-top cars, they were fitted with English Electric 305E motors and 4ft 9in bogies. English Electric Z6 controllers were fitted. In 1935, following extension of the check-rail, 'Luxury Dreadnoughts' were permitted to operate over the Clifton Drive-Cleveleys section from 8 June that year.

A further 20 railcoaches, Nos 264-83, were ordered in 1935 and delivered between June and September of that year. The Series 2 railcoaches differed only slightly from the earlier batch, but were fitted with English Electric 305E motors.

Thus, in the space of two years, Blackpool had received 84 new streamlined trams. Although this had allowed for the withdrawal of many of the older cars, including the original 'Dreadnoughts', the opportunity had also been taken to strengthen the operating fleet. There still remained a capacity problem on the Promenade route, which had been partially hidden through the operation of the blue trams of Lytham St Annes. However, the conversion of the Lytham system to bus operation during 1936 and 1937 meant that this additional capacity no longer existed. As a consequence, authorisation was given to acquire 20 new single-deck trams, Nos 284-303. Marshall had, by this date, left English Electric and was working as a consultant with, among others, Brush. The order, therefore, went to Loughborough and, although Brush retained the capacity to manufacture trams into the postwar era, the batch was destined to be the last the company manufactured.

As English Electric retained the patents for the original railcoach design, the Brush-built cars, whilst similar in outline, had detail differences. The bogies were EMB hornless 4ft 3in and the motors were Crompton Parkinson C162As rated at 57hp each. The controllers

motors rated at 40hp each. The seating capacity was 54 on the open top-deck and 40 in the lower saloon. The bodies were fitted with centre entrance/exit. Although open-top, No 226 entered service on 24 February; this was not as mad as it seemed since it was possible for the upper deck to be sealed off — allowing the car to operate as a conventional single-decker — with special holes in the staircases for rain water to drain away. In August 1934 No 226 was renumbered 237, allowing the production run of the 'Boats' to run in sequence from 225 to 236.

The 'Luxury Toastrack', No 225, was also fitted with a centre entrance/exit body. A total of 56 seats were provided in the two halves. Like the earlier railcoach, the 'Boat' was supplied with English Electric 4ft 0in bogies, although this car (and one other) was powered by two reconditioned Dick Kerr DK34B motors supplying 37hp each. The production batch of 'Boats' reached Blackpool in July and August 1934. Apart from No 226 (ii), which was fitted with Dick Kerr motors, the only significant changes from the prototype were the use of English Electric EE27A motors rated at 40hp each, slightly higher side panels and a different trolley arch. Nos 225 and 226 were fitted with reconditioned DB1-K44E controllers; the remainder of the batch received reconditioned BTH B18 controllers.

The production batch of open-top 'Luxury Dreadnoughts', Nos 238-49, started to arrive in September 1934 and, with the exception of were of the Crompton-West CTJ type. As with the English Electric cars, the bodies had centre entrance/exit, although these had air-operated doors rather than the manually-operated doors of the cars produced at Preston. Seating capacity, like all the other railcoaches was 48, with four folding seats (later removed) on the platform. The 20 cars entered service between July and October 1937.

Finally, a batch of 12 'Sun Saloons' was delivered between August and October 1939. Destined to replace the old 'Cross-Bench' cars Nos 126-40, these dozen cars were fitted with half-height windows, folding roofs, wooden seats and had no driver's partition. Supplied by English Electric, the cars reused BTH B265C motors from older cars and reconditioned English Electric DB1-K53E controllers. However, the delivery of the cars was overshadowed by events in central Europe — events which were to have a significant role in the future of Blackpool's streamlined trams.

The war brought changes to Blackpool and its trams. A fleet designed to cater for huge numbers of holiday-makers was ill suited to provide public transport throughout the whole year, particularly when the number of off-season passengers was destined to increase substantially. The number of passengers doubled between 1939 and 1943, and these problems were exacerbated by staff shortages (which prevented the operation of many trams) and by the requirement to operate special duties, such as the conveyance of troops to the ranges at Rossall. The cars allocated to this duty were drawn from Nos 10-21, and their rudimentary canvas roofs and half-height windows led to serious complaints. As a result, the entire batch was rebuilt with full-height windows, fixed roofs and driver's partitions during 1942. They were, however, to retain their wooden seats until further rebuilding after the war.

The 'Luxury Dreadnoughts' were also to receive treatment. From August 1941 (No 249) through to June 1942 (No 237), the entire batch was fitted with top covers, making them virtually identical to the earlier 'Balloons'. At the same time, the upper deck seating capacity was reduced to 44.

After the cessation of hostilities, attention turned again to the question of the Marton route. It had been planned that the route would have been modernised earlier, but the onset of war had caused a postponement. Elsewhere, similar delays were used as an excuse for abandonment; not so in Blackpool, where Walter Luff was still in control. In the period 1946-48 two of the prewar railcoaches, Nos 208 and 303, were subject to a series of tests. No 208 received Maley & Taunton HS44 6ft 0in bogies

A 'Boat' is delivered from the English Electric works at Preston in 1934. The car would be married with its English Electric 4ft 0in bogies at Rigby Road. A total of 12 'Boats' were supplied, of which six remain available for operation. *Ian Allan Library*

Above:
The prototype 'Luxury Dreadnought' No 226 was delivered in February 1934. Authorised in late 1933, No 226 and the prototype 'Boat' No 225 were as successful as the earlier English Electric 'Railcoaches' and bulk orders followed. In order to ensure continuity, No 226 was renumbered 237 in August 1934. Like the rest of the type, No 237 gained a fully enclosed top deck during World War 2. On the fleet renumbering in 1968 No 237 became No 700 and remains in service in 1993. *Ian Allan Library*

Below:
No 223 was the penultimate of a batch of 22 railcoaches, Nos 203-24, delivered in January-March 1934. This prewar shot illustrates the type's 4ft 0in English Electric bogies. No 223 was withdrawn in 1962, as the reduction in the size of the system led to a contraction in the fleet, and was scrapped in March 1963 at Marton depot. *R. Elliott*

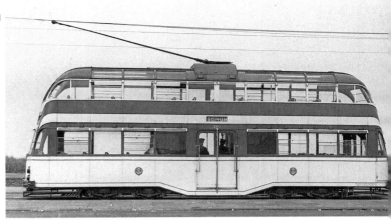

'Balloon' No 260, one of a batch of 14 fully enclosed double-deckers supplied in 1934-35, entered service in January 1935. This side view, taken when the car was almost new, shows in detail the English Electric 4ft 9in wheelbase trucks that were fitted to these cars and the arrangement of the green and cream livery. As No 723 this car remains in service in 1993. *R. Elliott*

with resilient wheels during 1946. These were, later the same year, replaced by a set of bogies with steel wheels and worm gears. It also received four Crompton Parkinson CP90A2 motors rated at 45hp each. In December Crompton Parkinson 'Vambac' control equipment was fitted. No 303 also received Maley & Taunton 6ft 0in bogies and four CP90A2 motors. Initially, it was fitted with CT/TJ controllers, but these were subsequently replaced by 'Vambac' equipment. Both cars were to receive modified HS44 bogies in 1952.

The 'Sun Saloons', Nos 10-21, underwent modification. Starting in January 1948, with No 10, the cars were progressively fitted with upholstered seats and fluorescent lighting. This programme of refurbishment continued

through until March 1951 when No 17 was so treated. However, for the last four cars, starting with No 20 in June 1950 and concluding with No 17, the refurbishment was extended to include the fitting of HS44 bogies and 'Vambac' control equipment. The first of the batch to be fitted with these modifications was No 21 in December 1949. The conversion was completed with No 13 in April 1952. Seventeen sets

Two of the English Electric railcoaches are seen at the South Shore (now Pleasure Beach) terminus alongside one of the small blue cars of Lytham St Annes Corporation heading south. Through services between the two seaside resorts ran until the final withdrawal of the blue trams in 1937. Proposals that Blackpool should take over the southern operation came to nothing. *A. D. Packer Collection*

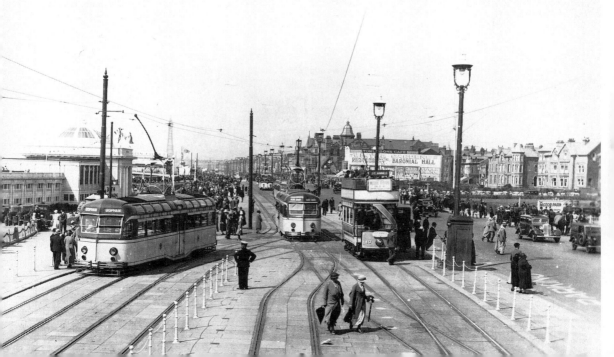

Above:
Brush-built railcoach No 292 heads north towards Fleetwood at Cleveleys on 9 September 1948. One of 20 cars that were to be the last manufactured by Brush, No 292 became No 629 in the 1968 renumbering. It was withdrawn in 1972 and scrapped in November the same year at Blundell Street depot. Although a number of these cars have been withdrawn (and one preserved), the majority were still in service in 1993.

Left:
'Boat' No 234 waits at 12.7pm on 9 September 1948 at Talbot Square — its destination — prior to heading south again. No 234 was new in August 1934 and was one of a number of the type withdrawn in 1963. Along with three other 'Boats' withdrawn at the same time it was stored at Blundell Street until April 1968 when they were all scrapped.

of HS44 bogies and allied equipment were ordered. Twelve of these were fitted to Nos 10-21, sets were also fitted to Nos 268 and 303 and the remaining sets were kept as spares. This meant that the Marton route, which required 15 cars to operate the peak service, only ever had a maximum of 14 'Vambac'-fitted cars. Equipment salvaged from Nos 10-21 was transferred to the older 'Pantograph' cars Nos 168-75.

The gradual introduction of the 'Vambac' controlled cars to the Marton route (the 12 ex-'Sun Saloons' and Nos 208 and 303) allowed for the withdrawal of several of the 'Standards' and 1954 was to see the last regular duties for those stalwarts of Blackpool's fleet. 14 October of the same year was to see the first operation, by No 259, of one of the streamlined double-deck cars on the Marton route. Earlier in the same year No 259 had appeared in a new livery of cream with green roof and waistband. Other cars, such as No 207, soon appeared in a similar style. By 1959, 21 of the double-deck cars had been painted in the new livery, leaving only Nos 242-44/46/48 in the older style.

Seen heading south from Cleveleys, No 204 was one of the original batch of English Electric Railcoaches supplied in January 1934. It was to last almost 30 years in service before withdrawal in 1963; it was scrapped at Thornton Gate sidings in October the same year.

'Luxury Dreadnought' No 246 is pictured at Little Bispham turning circle on 9 September 1948. Originally delivered in September 1934 as an open-top car, No 246 gained its top cover in November 1941. Becoming No 709 in the 1968 renumbering, the car remains in service in 1993.

The double-deck cars were also to get a modified destination display, with a single blind replacing the twin blinds of the original display. The first car so treated was No 256 in 1956. The process of modification continued over nearly 20 years! In mid-1957 a further modification saw the seating capacity on Nos 241/47/56 experimentally increased to 94; again other cars followed, the penultimate car to be treated being No 722 in mid-1992(!) leaving only No 720 as an 84-seater.

In 1957 work commenced on the conversion of two of the railcoaches, Nos 275 and 276, as the prototype twin-car set. The cars remained largely as original, except for the adoption of 'Coronation'-style driver's cabs. The original English Electric bogies were retained. No 275 was the trailer unit and, although the driver's cabs were retained to facilitate future reconversion, driving was possible only from No 276. The twin-set was fitted with a Willison automatic coupler and Westinghouse airbrakes. The twin-set made its first run on 18 January 1958, proudly announcing itself as the 'Progress Twin Car'. The trailer unit was first used in service on 9 April 1958 and first appeared on the Promenade route on 24 May of the same year.

The success of the prototype set led the Transport Committee to authorise the purchase of 10 trailers, Nos T1-T10, from MCW on 13 March 1959. Each trailer was to cost £4,883, with the trucks from Maley & Taunton to cost an additional £2,797 per pair. The cars were ordered in June 1959 and deliveries started in July 1960. The first was formally handed over on 19 July, when No 277 and No T1 took an official party on a tour of the system. The last two were delivered in January 1961. The trailers were 43ft 10in in length with a seating capacity of 66. They were delivered in the new cream livery with green band. No 275 entered Rigby Road Works on 3 November 1960 for reconversion into a power car.

In order to haul the new trailers, eight more of the railcoaches were converted in a similar way to No 276. These were Nos 272-74/77-81 and the work took until May 1962. Initially, the driving cars retained their cabs at both ends, but eventually the majority of the twin-sets were permanently coupled and one driver's cab and equipment was transferred to the trailer. Once completed, the twin-sets operated as Nos 271+T1 through to 280+T10.

Just as the winds of change had affected other 'secure' tramway systems, so Blackpool itself underwent a crisis in the early 1960s, with the conversion of the three remaining town routes. The first route to succumb, on 29 October 1961, was that to Squires Gate via Lytham Road. No 268 departed from Squires Gate terminus at 11.45pm, making it the last car to operate over the route. The next route to be converted was that to Marton. Despite the investment barely a decade earlier and the opposition of local ratepayers, the Marton route was converted on 28 October 1962. Of the Marton 'Vambacs', Nos 11/13/15/17/18 were available for use at the end; of the remainder Nos 10 and 21 had already been scrapped and the rest were partially dismantled. No 11 was sold for preservation and departed for Havant on 9 September 1965. After a short stay in Hampshire, the car migrated to the East Anglian Transport Museum at Carlton Colville in January 1969. Following the withdrawal, 17 cars, including Nos 12-20 and 303, were sold for scrap and dismantled in Marton depot. The final closure took place on 27 October 1963 when the North Station-Dickson Road route was converted and No 290 was the last service car on the route.

The closures of the early 1960s meant that Blackpool now had a significant surplus of trams and a number of the streamlined cars were to be withdrawn during the period. The withdrawals included the prototype No 200 which was scrapped in March 1963 and the rest of the 1933-34 batch of railcoaches were withdrawn between 1961 and 1965, with the exception of No 224. All were scrapped with the exception of No 209 which was used to form the basis of the Santa Fe illuminated tram (later No 733); No 219, which was stored and eventually rebuilt as OMO (One Man Operation) car No 4; No 221, which became Permanent Way car No 5 and later OMO No 5; and No 222, which was used as the basis for the illuminated Hovertram (later No 735). The one survivor of the batch, renumbered 610 and latterly used as a Permanent Way gang car in place of No 170, was withdrawn in 1969 and later converted to OMO No 3. Also withdrawn were four of the 'Boats', Nos 229/31/32/34.

Although there were fears for the future of the Promenade route, these were largely unfounded. A further change of livery in early 1964 saw Nos 269/85/88/90/91/96/99, 300 and 301 appear with cream below the waist band and green above and by later the same year all the remaining Brush-built cars, and Nos 269 and 270, had been similarly treated.

In early 1965, the first semi-permanent trailer units were formed with the modification to Nos 271+T1-274+T4. The work involved transferring the No 2 driving end from the motor

tram to the trailer car. At the same time the four sets were painted in the new half cream/half green livery. Other sets followed: Nos 275+T5 in early 1966; Nos 276+T6 (by then renumbered 676/86) in mid-1969; and Nos 277+T7 (Nos 677/87) in late 1969. Another new departure was the application of fleet numbers to the front of the trams; the first to so appear being Brush-built Nos 290/96.

Starting on 29 November 1965 double-deck cars were used on test workings for a period to see if there was any need for double-deck duties during the winter timetable. Three cars, Nos 240/57/63, were run but the results showed that there was not the demand, and the experiment was not repeated.

More positive was the emergence, on 13 January 1966, of the rebuilt railcoach No 264. The car had been involved in a minor accident and had been stored. The opportunity was taken to rebuild the car. Using the fibre glass front-ends originally destined for the unbuilt 11th and 12th trailer cars, and wind-

In 1966 No 264, the first of the Series 2 Railcoaches, was rebuilt using plastic panelling and fitted with front ends similar to those used on the twin-sets. The rebuilt car was, at 42ft 8in, six inches longer than when new. The use of the plastic panels was an attempt to solve the problem caused by Blackpool's climate to the traditional paint finish on the trams. No 264 became No 611 under the 1968 renumbering scheme and was withdrawn in 1974. Following rebuilding, the car emerged as OMO car No 12 in June 1975. *ICI plastics*

screens salvaged from the now withdrawn 'Coronation' car No 313, a tram similar to the twin-cars was produced. Apart from interior refurbishment, the work also included the fitting of plastic panels on the exterior, in order to reduce the damage to bodywork caused by operating in a corrosive environment. The new car was also slightly longer (at 43ft 9in) than its original 42ft 3in.

At the end of 1968 Blackpool undertook its first ever fleet renumbering. All the surviving streamlined single-deck cars were numbered in the 600-90 series and the double-deckers in the 700-26 range. The twin-sets were numbered 671-80 (power cars) and 681-90 (trailers). The illuminated cars became Nos 731-36 and, in 1972, the works cars became Nos 749/50/52-54. At this date there remained eights 'Boats', one of the first series of railcoaches, eight of the 1935 batch (including the rebuilt No 264), the 10 rebuilt twin-set power cars, 20 of the Brush-built cars and all the 'Balloons'.

A second rebuilt Series 2 railcoach, No 618, appeared in January 1969. This car was fitted with tapered ends and had its seating capacity increased from 48 to 56. It was also painted in the half cream/half green livery. This was followed in late 1969 by the fitting of front entrances to Brush-built No 638 for OMO experiments. No 638's seating capacity was, as a result, reduced to 44 with 20 standing. It was fitted with power-operated folding doors and was painted in an all-cream livery. It did not enter service until mid-1970.

On 28 September 1969 Nos 628 and 726 collided. This led to the withdrawal of No 628. In late 1970 work started on converting the frames of the car into a new engineering car (No 751). Late 1970 also saw the operation of Nos 678-80 without trailers over the winter period. These three sets were now the only three that had not been converted into permanent twin-sets. Although reunited with trailers for use in the summer season that year, Nos 688-90 were withdrawn from stock in 1972. Whilst No 688 remains 'in stock', Nos 689 and 690 were sold to GEC for experimental purposes in November 1981. When GEC had completed their work, both were sold to the West Yorkshire Transport Museum in November 1984. Unfortunately, pressure on the museum meant that both were eventually dismantled.

In early 1971 'Boat' No 601 was experimentally fitted with a pantograph; later it reverted to normal trolleypole operation and was sold to the Rio Vista Museum in California in August the same year. Also in early 1971 No 611 received the illuminated roof advertising panels from 'Coronation' No 658. As other 'Coronation'

cars were withdrawn so they also surrendered the advertising panels to the earlier railcoaches.

The autumn of 1971 was to witness the next major development when authorisation was given to build new bodies for OMO use. The cars selected for treatment were Nos 610/16/17/20 along with Nos PW5 and 220. The first rebuilt car was presented to the Transport Committee on 7 March 1972 in a bright new 'sunshine and crimson' livery. The cars were 49ft long and could seat 50 with 16 standing. The seating capacity was later reduced to 48. Although the first completed car emerged as No 616, it was soon renumbered No 1. Authorisation for a further seven conversions was given later in the year and the last of the type, No 13, entered service in June 1976. Due to the increased length of the OMO cars, it proved necessary to fit them with slightly longer trolleypoles.

During the four year programme for the building of the OMO cars, there were a number of alterations to the type. Of these the most important were the adoption of 'Metalastik' suspension from No 10 onwards (which proved remarkably successful, increasing tyre life from 60,000 miles to 100,000) and the changed red and cream livery that also first appeared on the completion of No 10 in April 1975. In early 1976 three of the cars, Nos 4, 5 and 13, were fitted with pantographs, following trials with No 678 in the previous year. The initial tests were not wholly successful and the cars reverted to trolley pole operation.

Series 2 Railcoach No 613 heads towards Talbot Square over one of the few sections of traditional street tramway to survive in Blackpool on 20 May 1972. The fitting of illuminated roof panels (and later the appearance of trams in overall advertisement liveries) was a means by which additional revenue could be brought in at a time when passenger revenue was in decline. No 613 was to be withdrawn the following year and rebuilt as OMO car No 9. *R. E. Ruffell*

With the OMO programme proceeding, experimental car No 638 had its front entrances removed and reverted to a two-man vehicle in the green/cream livery in late 1974. Other Brush-built cars (Nos 622/23/27/31/34/37) were modified by mid-1977 with the replacement of their existing controllers by English Electric DB1Z6 controllers recovered from scrapped 'Coronation' cars. Others had, by now, been withdrawn, including No 635 (in 1974) which was preserved. Prior to preservation No 635 was fitted with Crompton Parkinson C162A motors (in place of English Electric EE305s fitted in 1965) and Allen West CT/TJ controllers.

Whilst these developments were taking place, behind the scenes work was progressing on the construction of a 'new' double-deck tram, No 761. Two of the 'Balloons', Nos 714 and 725, had been withdrawn in 1971 and these formed the basis of two new cars. No 761 (formerly No 725) was officially launched on 4 July 1979. The body was built around the original teak framing of the original car, with extensions provided by Metal Sections. The actual construction was handled in Rigby Road depot. The original bogies were substantially rebuilt to allow for a 5ft 6in wheelbase and the use of 'Metalastik' suspension. Westinghouse chopper control was adopted although the original EE305 motors were retained. The body was provided with a single forward entrance, which proved a cause of significant delays when in service. Although initially provided with 100 sets, this number was later reduced to 98 in order to increase circulating area. Fitted successfully with a pantograph, the car entered full OMO service on 25 February 1980.

With the completion of No 761, work started on the conversion of No 714. The car was completed by early 1982 and was on test in April of that year. It was formally inspected by Department of Transport inspectors on 27 May 1982. Largely similar to No 761, the most significant variation is the retention of the centre entrance/exit to improve passenger flow, which reduces the seating capacity to 90 (56 in the upper saloon and 34 in the lower).

On 22 July 1980 two other 'Balloons', Nos 705 and 706, were withdrawn as a result of a collision. No 705 was sold for scrap (to Lister of Bolton) in August 1982 and dismantled at Blundell Street depot in October of that year. The trucks were passed to the Merseyside Transport Preservation Society and certain spares were retained for the rebuilding of No 706. The restoration of No 706, which included rebuilding it back to near original open-top condition and the fitting of a panto-

graph, was completed in time for the car to appear in the 1985 centenary celebrations. By this date pantographs were appearing on an increasing number of cars; by mid-1985 other cars so fitted included OMO cars Nos 1/3/5/7-10 and 'Balloons' Nos 712 and 719, plus the two rebuilt double-deckers.

In late 1982 a further livery change saw No 701 emerge in a new mainly cream livery and other trams soon adopted the new style. In mid-1984 OMO No 1 appeared in a new cream livery with green waistband and the bulk of the type followed, although the last of the type,

Right:
Although the majority of the 'Balloons' remain in service, one has been scrapped and two, Nos 714 and 725, have been rebuilt. With a body constructed by Blackpool Corporation and Metal Sections, No 761 was reconstructed from No 725 and entered service in 1979. The front entrance/exit led to relatively slow loading and unloading and on No 762 the traditional centre entrance/exit was retained. *Michael Dryhurst*

Below:
The first of the OMO cars, No 1, appeared in October 1972 and a total of 13 were produced between then and June 1976. The first livery adopted for the type was a somewhat garish yellow and red combination. From No 10, in 1975, the cars were delivered in a red and white livery, which survived until 1984 when No 1, as pictured here, appeared in the new white and green livery launched by the 'Centenary' class car No 641. No 1 was originally Series 2 Railcoach No 269 (616). The car was finally withdrawn in 1989, although, at the time of writing, its remains survive at Rigby Road depot. *W. J. Haynes*

No 13, was soon to be withdrawn. After cannibalisation for spares, No 13 was dismantled on 23 March 1985 — the first of the type to be withdrawn.

Other events of this period saw the scrapping of No 638 in 1983 and the restoration to service, after a period as a driver training car, of No 637. In early 1984 No 710 was loaned to the National Tramway Museum in replacement for a number of historical cars loaned to Blackpool in the build-up to the centenary year of 1985. In late 1984 'Boat' No 600 was loaned to Heaton Park (Manchester), whilst sister car No 605 was restored to 1934 condition. A third 'Boat', No 603, which had been withdrawn in 1975 and loaned to Philadelphia in 1976 (for which it had been regauged to 1,580mm), returned to the USA in February 1985, where it is now preserved at El Paso. Finally, again for the duration of the centenary, No 607 was loaned to Crich. Both Nos 607 and 710 returned to Blackpool in December 1985. A further loan, in 1988, saw 'Boat' No 606 loaned to Glasgow for that city's very successful garden festival.

The centenary year, 1985, was marked by the introduction of a new class of single-deck tram — the 'Centenary' class — built by East Lancs, and the gradual introduction of the new class of eight (eventually) allowed for the gradual withdrawal of the OMO cars. These cars, which had given sterling service, were increasingly to suffer from body sag. Following on from No 13, Nos 2 and 4 were to be withdrawn in 1985. These were followed by Nos 3 and 7; the latter car was stripped down in early 1987 and formed the basis of a replica 'toastrack' car, No 619, which entered service on 14 September 1987. The next two to be withdrawn were Nos 6 and 9 at the end of 1987. This left only No 12 in the old red and cream livery; the remaining cars, Nos 1/5/8/10/11 were either in the cream/green livery, or in the case of No 10 in an all-over advertisement livery.

By late 1990 both Nos 1 and 12 were also withdrawn and the opportunity was taken to replace the BTH B18 controllers on three 'Boats', Nos 602/4/5, with English Electric Z4 or Z6 controllers salvaged from scrapped OMO cars by mid-1992. No 1, finally scrapped in 1991, bequeathed its trucks to No 680. No 8 was withdrawn in mid-1992, leaving only Nos 5/10/11 in service; the future for these remaining OMO cars is uncertain, although No 5 was refurbished in 1991. Although the OMO cars may only have a short future (indeed reports of their final demise were appearing as this chapter was being written), other types continue to see work undertaken on them — the fitting of pantographs to Nos 602 and 604 (although this was not successful and all have reverted to conventional trolleypole operation) and the repainting of No 701 in a pre-1930 style red livery being but two examples.

The story of the Blackpool streamliners is now exactly 60 years old. Few classes of tram have lasted as long or have undergone so many changes. That the cars have survived and played a fundamental role in the continuing story of the Blackpool system is a tribute both to the original concept of Walter Luff and to the workmanship of the original manufacturers. Of the 100 or so cars built between 1933 and 1939 well over half survive, in some form, to continue the story into the 1990s.

Following accident damage in 1984, 'Balloon' No 706 was rebuilt back to an open-top condition similar to that in which it was originally delivered. It is seen here in Manchester Square on 27 May 1985. It is interesting to compare it with the earlier photograph of No 226 when new in 1934. *David A. Ingham*

The second of the rebuilt double-deck trams, No 762, appeared in April 1982. Following problems with handling the Promenade crowds on the single-door No 761, this car retained a centre entrance. This meant that the seating capacity was only 90, in comparison with No 761's 98. *Ian Allan Library*

The Blackpool 'Streamlined' Cars

Number	New	1968 number	Withdrawn	Fate
200	June 1933	—	1962	Scr March 1963
201	December 1933	—	1963	Scr September 1963
202	December 1933	—	1963	Scr September 1963
203	January 1934	—	1962	Scr December 1962
204	January 1934	—	1962	Scr October 1963
205	January 1934	—	1962	Scr July 1963
206	January 1934	—	1961	Scr December 1961
207	January 1934	—	1962	Scr March 1963
208	January 1934	—	1962	Scr March 1963
209	January 1934	—	1962	Frame/Trucks to No 733
210	January 1934	—	1962	Scr March 1963
211	January 1934	—	1965	Scr October 1965
212	January 1934	—	1965	Scr October 1965
213	January 1934	—	1965	Scr October 1965
214	January 1934	—	1962	Scr March 1963
215	January 1934	—	1963	Scr November 1963
216	February 1934	—	1965	Scr October 1965
217	February 1934	—	1965	Scr October 1965
218	February 1934	—	1963	Scr September 1963
219	February 1934	—	1962	Scr July 1963
220	February 1934	—	1963	Stored until 1972 then OMO No 4
221	February 1934	—	1965	PWD No 5 April 1965 then OMO No 5

222	February 1934	—	1963	Frame/Trucks to Hovertram (No 735)
223	February 1934	—	1962	Scr March 1963
224	May 1934	610	1969	To OMO No 3
225	February 1934	600		
226 (ii)	August 1934	601	1970	Preserved USA
227	July 1934	602		
228	July 1934	603	1979	Preserved USA
229	July 1934	—	1963	Scr April 1968
230	August 1934	604		
231	August 1934	—	1963	Scr April 1968
232	August 1934	—	1963	Scr April 1968
233	August 1934	605		
234	August 1934	—	1963	Scr April 1968
235	August 1934	606		
236	August 1934	607		
237*	February 1934	700		
238	September 1934	701		
239	September 1939	702		
240	September 1934	703		
241	September 1934	704		
242	September 1934	705	July 1980	Scr October 1982
243	September 1934	706	July 1980**	Restored 1985
244	September 1934	707		
245	September 1934	708		
246	September 1934	709		
247	October 1934	710		
248	October 1934	711		
249	October 1934	712		
250	December 1934	713		
251	December 1934	714	1971	Rebuilt as No 762
252	January 1935	715		
253	February 1935	716		
254	December 1934	717		
255	December 1934	718		
256	February 1935	719		
257	February 1935	720		
258	March 1935	721		
259	February 1935	722		
260	January 1935	723		
261	February 1935	724		
262	January 1935	725	1971	Rebuilt as No 761
263	February 1935	726		
264	June 1935	611	1974	To OMO No 12
265	June 1935	612	1972	To OMO No 8
266	June 1935	613	1973	To OMO No 9
267	June 1935	614	1973	To OMO No 10
268	June 1935	615	1974	To OMO No 11
269	July 1935	616	1970	To OMO No 1
270	July 1935	617	1972	To OMO No 6
271	July 1935	618	1975	To OMO No 13
272	July 1935	672		Rebuilt September 1960
273	July 1935	673		Rebuilt June 1961
274	July 1935	674		Rebuilt May 1962
275	July 1935	675		Rebuilt April 1958
276	July 1935	676		Rebuilt April 1958
277	July 1935	677		Rebuilt July 1960
278	July 1935	678		Rebuilt September 1961

279	July 1935	679		Rebuilt April 1961
280	July 1935	680		Rebuilt December 1960
281	July 1935	671		Rebuilt November 1960
282	August 1935	619	1972	To OMO No 7
283	September 1935	620	1970	To OMO No 2
284	July 1937	621		
285	July 1937	622		
286	July 1937	623		
287	July 1937	624	1971	To PWD No 748
288	July 1937	625		
289	August 1937	626		
290	August 1937	627		
291	August 1937	628	1969	To PWD No 751
292	August 1937	629	1972	Scr November 1972
293	August 1937	630		
294	August 1937	631		
295	August 1937	632		
296	August 1937	633		
297	September 1937	634		
298	September 1937	635	1974	Preserved
299	September 1937	636		
300	September 1937	637	(1982)	Reinstated 1985
301	September 1937	—	1966	Scr April 1968
302	October 1937	638	1980	Scr 1983
303	October 1937	—	1962	Scr March 1963
10	August 1939	—	1958	Scr February 1961
11	August 1939	—	1962	Preserved
12	August 1939	—	1962	Scr March 1963
13	September 1939	—	1962	Scr March 1963
14	August 1939	—	1962	Scr March 1963
15	August 1939	—	1962	Scr March 1963
16	September 1939	—	1962	Scr March 1963
17	September 1939	—	1962	Scr March 1963
18	October 1939	—	1962	Scr March 1963
19	October 1939	—	1962	Scr March 1963
20	October 1939	—	1962	Scr March 1963
21	October 1939	—	1962	Scr March 1963

Notes:
* Originally No 226 (i) until August 1934.
** No 706 stored following collision with No 705; rebuilt in open-top form 1985.

OMO Cars

Number	Old Number	To service	Withdrawn	Fate
1	616	October 1972	1989	Remains stored
2	620	October 1972	1985	Scr 1987
3	610	October 1972	1987	Scr 1987
4	220	October 1972	1985	Scr 1987
5	PWD 5/221	November 1972	1993	Stored
6	617	April 1973	1987	Scr 1988
7	619	July 1973	1987	Rebuilt as No 619
8	612	August 1974	1992	Remains stored
9	613	December 1974	1987	Scr 1988
10	614	April 1975	1993	Stored
11	615	May 1975	1993	Stored
12	611	June 1975	1988	Remains stored
13	618	June 1976	1985	Scr March 1985

7.

The Belfast 'McCreary' Cars

The city of Belfast possessed a substantial electric tramway until 1954. It was constructed to the unusual gauge of 4ft 9in and was to see considerable investment right through until the mid-1930s, when the 50 'McCreary' cars were to become the last new trams delivered to the city.

In 1931 William Chamberlain, General Manager since November 1928, resigned to join the Traffic Commissioners in London. He was succeeded by Lt-Col Robert McCreary, who had been employed by the Transport Department since 1919. Prior to his war service, McCreary had been employed in the Surveyor's Department where his work had included, *inter alia*, the 1913 tramway extensions.

McCreary inherited a fleet of some 390 cars. Of these the majority were 'Standard Reds' constructed between 1905 and 1910, although these had been modified and some 50 had been extensively rebuilt as 'DK1s' in 1929. There was also a batch of 50 cars that were nominally rebuilds of earlier horse trams. Between 1920 and 1930 a total of 100 new cars were built — the 50 'Moffett' cars and the 50 'Chamberlains'. However, by the mid-1930s the need to replace some of the old ex-horse trams and early 'Standard Reds' was becoming pressing.

In late 1934 authorisation was given for the construction of 50 new cars. These were designed by English Electric at Preston to the outline specification produced by McCreary. The first car, No 392, was unveiled in early 1935 and, with its streamlined design, was in marked contrast to the traditional design of the Chamberlains'. The four-wheel truck was a Maley & Taunton 8ft 0in swinglink and the all-metal body was supplied by English Electric. The car was 32ft 0in in length. Electrical equipment, including two 50hp motors, was supplied by Crompton Parkinson. The controllers were either Metro-Vick OK27Bs or OK34Bs. Seating accommodation was provided for 40 in the upper saloon — in two-by-two transverse seating — and for 24 in the lower — with two-by-one transverse seats. All seats were upholstered. The blue livery, with cream relief, was adopted by Chamberlain on No 164 in 1929 to differentiate those trams with upholstered seats from those, which retained the red livery, without such luxury. Segregated driving cabs were provided on this car (and on No 393), but this feature was not perpetuated on the remaining 48. Double folding doors were also provided. The cars were also well provided with both front and side destination blinds and route number boxes.

The first of the cars entered service in April 1935 and the remaining 49 were introduced over the next year. Underframes for 30 of the cars — the order for this part of the batch had been increased from 20 to 30 in February 1935 — were supplied by Hurst Nelson of Motherwell to Service Motor Works in Belfast for the construction of the body. Service Motor Works had undertaken a significant amount of work earlier for the Corporation, including building the last 10 of the 'Chamberlains' and in the rebuilding of the 'DK1s'. The Belfast-built cars became Nos 393-422.

Following experience with the first five cars, which suffered from drooped platforms, the remaining underframes were strengthened. The modification, was not, however, wholly successful. The construction of the 50 new cars allowed for a number of older cars to be withdrawn. It has been suggested that the inherent structural weakness of the cars was one factor in their relatively early demise, with the older 'Chamberlains' being preferred in the final stages of the abandonment programme.

Above:
Apart from the 'Standard Reds', the Belfast fleet also comprised initially a number of cars, Nos 201-50, that were nominally rebuilds of horse trams. A number of these were eventually fitted with top-covers, but a number, such as No 247, remained open-top throughout their career — probably the last cars so built to remain operational in a major city. A number survived into the postwar years and must have been a curious contrast to the modern 'McCreary' cars. *F. N. T. Lloyd Jones/Courtesy A. D. Packer*

Below:
Pictured at the Ballygomartin terminus is 'Standard Red' No 120 dating from 1905 in the red and white livery, whilst on the right is 'McCreary' No 420, one of the Service Motor Works-built cars. *R. C. Ludgate*

The remaining 19 cars, No 423-41 were constructed by English Electric. Although to the same basic design, there were slight detail variations between the two manufacturers' work; for example, the headlight in the English Electric-built cars was slightly higher in the dash than that on the Service Motor Works-built examples.

In 1937 six of the 'McCreary' cars (Nos 426/27/29/31/33/34) were painted in a special red, white and blue livery to mark the Coronation of King George VI. But, by this date, a decision had been taken which was to determine the ultimate fate of the tramway system. In October 1936 the Transport Committee decided, following the powers permitted within the 1930 Belfast Corporation Act, to introduce trolleybuses. The first route to be trolleybus operated was that along the Falls Road, which saw the first trolleybuses introduced on 28 March 1938. In January 1939 the decision was made to convert the remaining tram routes over a five-year period.

The outbreak of war in September 1939 was to render such a time scale impractical, although the trolleybus system was significantly extended during the period with the conversion of six routes between September 1940 and March 1943. For the 'McCreary' cars, and the bulk of the fleet, the war meant a temporary reprieve, although many of the cars were to suffer slight damage during the bombing raids that the city suffered. There was, however, to be one significant modification to the cars. The double transverse seat in the lower saloon was replaced by a longitudinal seat in order to increase the number of standing passengers that could be accommodated. In 1944 a revised, austerity, livery (of the normal blue and cream but without lining) appeared. A number of cars, including No 439, ran in this livery.

After the cessation of hostilities, although conversion remained the long term aim, the immediate priority was to get the system operating properly. To this end a considerable amount of track work repairs was undertaken and many cars, including Nos 396/98, 403/04/21/25, were overhauled and repainted during 1945. By August 1945 all the Belfast fleet

Above:
The first of the 'McCreary' cars, No 392, pictured when new looking immaculate in its blue and white livery with elaborate gold lining out. When delivered the cars had white roofs, but, after a few years service, these were repainted blue. No 392 was built by English Electric and, like No 393, was provided with a separate driver's cab. *R. C. Ludgate Collection*

Below:
No 393 was the first of the batch produced by Service Motor Works. It differed from the remainder of these locally-built cars in being fitted with separate driver's cabs. Comparison with the previous photograph illustrates the minor variation of the front end treatment between the EE and SMW-built cars. *W. J. Haynes*

Left:
The upper saloon of one of the 'McCreary' cars showing clearly the two-by-two transverse seats and the lack of an internal bulkhead. *The Electric Railway, Bus and Tram Journal*

Below left:
The lower saloon of a 'McCreary' car. The twin transverse seats were removed during World War 2 and replaced by longitudinal seating in order to increase the overall capacity. *The Electric Railway, Bus and Tram Journal*

had lost their blackout markings; gradually normality was returning.

During the late 1940s, whilst work continued on repairing certain routes and on overhauling the fleet (Nos 405/26/31, for example being treated in mid-1947), the gradual conversion programme continued. Between January 1945 and January 1949 a total of six routes were converted to either trolleybus or bus operation, although in 1948 the trams still carried more than half the total number of passengers in the city. At this time the 'McCreary' cars were used widely throughout the remaining system, such as the routes to Greencastle and Ligoniel.

In 1947, after the tragic fire at Green Lane depot in Liverpool, Belfast offered a number of the 'McCreary' cars to the English city to replace those trams damaged. The offer was declined because of the difference in gauge, although as proved elsewhere, this need not have been a major barrier if the authorities in Liverpool had been less eager to see the Edge Lane fire as a blessing in disguise for the city's abandonment programme.

By early 1950 a total of 200 cars remained in service. These included all the earlier 'Moffett'

and 'Chamberlain' cars as well as all 50 of the 'McCreary' class. All were based at either Ardoyne or Mountpottinger depots by the end of that year. By this date the conversion programme had resulted in the withdrawal of the last of the ex-horse cars (although one was to survive into preservation) and the majority of 'Standard Reds'. However, on 13 November 1950 No 414 was severely damaged in a collision with an empty coal train at the junction of Old Channel Road and Queen's Road. As the tram was empty there were no casualties, but the tram was stored whilst a decision was made as to its future. Inevitably, given the gradual conversion programme, the car was not destined to operate again and it was finally scrapped on 19 September 1951.

This casualty was, however, balanced by the re-entry to service in December 1950 of No 399 which had been out of action for some time with a defective motor. It was repaired with a motor salvaged from No 414 following the latter's accident. Conversely, less positive was the fact that in April 1950 Nos 392 and 431 were overhauled and completely repainted — these were probably the last cars so treated.

The next casualty was also unplanned. On 18 February 1951 a fire broke out at Ardoyne depot and three cars ('Moffett' No 326, 'Chamberlain' No 372 and 'McCreary' No 396) were destroyed. The remains of all three cars were consigned to the Permanent Way Yard at Mountpottinger on Monday 19 February for scrap. A further four cars ('DK1' No 282, 'Chamberlains' Nos 374 and 386, and 'McCreary' No 438) were seriously damaged and placed in store at Shore Road whilst their future was considered. Five cars, including 'McCreary' cars Nos 399 and 418, were repaired. It is believed that the fire was the result of a short circuit in one of the three cars destroyed.

Apart from the two casualties — Nos 396 and 414 — all the class remained in stock in April 1951. Between August 1950 and November 1951 a further five routes had been converted. By this date Robert McCreary had resigned — to be replaced by Joseph Mackle, the Rolling Stock Engineer who had been act-

During 1938 Belfast introduced its first trolleybuses on the route to Falls Road, the start of a major conversion programme to this form of transport. Two of the Service Motor Works-built 'McCreary' cars, Nos 406 nearest the camera and 402, are seen alongside one of the new AEC 664T trolleybuses delivered between 1940 and 1943 as further tram routes were converted. The Cregagh route was converted during 1941 and this photograph must date from around that time — witness the shaded headlights, the white bumpers and the number of people in uniform. *Ian Allan Library*

ing Deputy General Manager between 1940 and 1945. After his retirement, McCreary was to act as a consultant to Dundee and it was to be his report that led to the abandonment of that Scottish city's system in 1955-56.

In early 1952 No 420 was withdrawn in order to provide a source of spares for the remaining cars. This was the first casualty amongst the type other than for fire or accident reasons. A total of 20 route miles remained operational, although this was to be soon reduced further. In November 1952 a further four routes were converted and this resulted in the withdrawal of several cars, including a further 'McCreary' No 403. By early 1953 withdrawal of the type accelerated. In June and July of that year seven of the type were withdrawn and scrapped —

Below:
'McCreary' car No 431, one of the 20 of the type built by English Electric, is seen at the Springfield Road terminus as the conductor turns the trolleypole prior to departure back to Ballygomartin. The Springfield-Ballygomartin route was converted to bus operation on 9 November 1952. In the background can be seen 'Chamberlain' car No 364, one of a batch of 50 cars built by Brush and Service Motor Works in 1930, which were the immediate predecessors of the 'McCreary' cars. *R. C. Ludgate*

English Electric-built 'McCreary' No 427 heads past Ardoyne depot *en route* to the city centre on route No 57.
R. C. Ludgate

Nos 392/4, 400/13/15/19/28 — leaving 39 in service out of a total fleet of 126. Although the conversion programme was running behind schedule, the city's Lord Mayor was able to comment that the opening of the new Short Strand bus depot on 15 June was the 'beginning of the last stage of the tramway era in Belfast'.

The prototype car, No 392, was to be the next casualty, being withdrawn on 16 June 1953 following severe damage from a fire caused by overheating resistances on the No 1 end. The car was scrapped a week later.

In September a further five 'McCreary' cars — Nos 395, 412/17/18/35 — were taken out of service and on 10 and 11 October 1953 all remaining all-day services were withdrawn from the last tram routes (Ligoniel via Crumlin Road or Shankill Road, and Queen's Road). For the system's last few months trams were to be limited to peak hour services only.

Late 1953 saw the demise of a further batch of the type — Nos 423/25/27/29-33. The remaining cars were not to operate again in public service after mid-November and, whilst 10 remained in stock at closure, on 28 February 1954 none was to feature in the actual closure procession. All 50 of the type were to be scrapped, being dismantled at Mountpottinger depot. Of Belfast's electric tramcar fleet, only two survive: one of the converted horse trams (No 249) and a 'Chamberlain' (No 357).

Two of the EE-built cars, Nos 419 and 434, are seen at the Balmoral terminus in the early 1950s. The Balmoral service was converted to bus operation on 9 November 1952.
R. C. Ludgate

8

The Liverpool 'Streamliners'

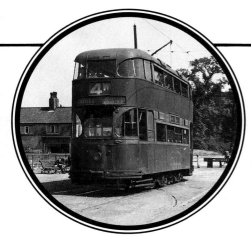

The City of Liverpool had, during the 1920s and 1930s, one of the most progressive of all Britain's tramway systems. A great investment went into the building of new tram routes — mostly on segregated reservations — and on the modernisation of the tramcar fleet. The latter work included both the reconstruction of older cars and the building of more than 400 trams from 1930 through to 1942. Of these 163 were bogie streamlined cars (Nos 151-88 and 868-992) and 100 (Nos 201-300) were streamlined four-wheelers built between 1936 and 1942.

The modernisation of the Liverpool system and in particular the construction of the streamlined cars owed much to the appointment of W. G. Marks as General Manager. Marks' background had seen him act as General Manager at both Chesterfield and Nottingham and in both places he had shown himself to be keen on the development of the trolleybus. There were those, therefore, that viewed his arrival in Liverpool in February 1934 as ushering in an age of trolleybus conversion in the city. This was not to be, however, as Marks with his team of engineers set to work on the development of modern trams for the city. Such was Marks' advocacy of the tram that he was to become ultimately the president of the Light Railway Transport League; a position that he felt constrained to resign from after the war, when the authorities in Liverpool rejected any further investment in the tramway network in favour of abandonment.

When appointed Marks believed that the system required around 300 modern, fast trams with a high seating capacity. The first designs appeared in January 1935 and in February the Corporation agreed on a modernisation plan. Authorisation was given to building 50 cars on 31 July 1935. By this date R. J. Heathman, who

had been employed by English Electric, was appointed Engineering Draughstman and this may help to explain why certain design features of the Blackpool streamlined cars appeared in the Liverpool ones.

On 8 October 1935, following successful tests under No 809, 50 sets of EMB Lightweight bogies of type L5 were ordered. GEC was to supply the motors and Metro-Vick was to provide the control equipment. In June 1936 the first of the new cars (No 868), with bodywork built at Edge Lane — the Corporation's own workshops — appeared. The new car was 39ft 9in long and 7ft 4in wide. It could accommodate 44 passengers in the upper saloon (all transverse) and 34 in the lower (24 transverse and 10 longitudinal) with the capacity for an additional six standing passengers. The new car also introduced a new livery variant. The olive green livery had been originally adopted in the early 1930s and had been modified with the addition of extra ivory soon after. With No 868 the ivory was extended to two wide bands surrounding the windows of both decks.

The body was of composite construction with aluminium panels over a wooden frame. EMB-supplied 'Joburg' radial-arm bogies were fitted to Nos 868-78/80 whilst the Lightweight bogies (classified LW2 in Liverpool to differentiate them from the earlier LW1) were fitted to the remaining 38 cars of the first batch (Nos 879/81-917). All were fitted with four GEC WT181AS motors, rated at 40hp, with the exception of No 905, which received four Crompton Parkinson C190A motors, rated at 34hp each. (No 905 was to receive WT181AS motors in 1952; it was also fitted experimentally from 1936-38 with a Crompton Parkinson control panel as the company sought to regain its traditional market in Liverpool.) The motors cost £560 per car. Electropneumatic control, fitted with miniature master controllers, was also supplied.

The next batch of 25 cars was to mark another change; this time the work for the bogies was to be placed with Maley & Taunton. The bogies, along with the associated control equipment from Metro-Vick and GEC motors, were ordered in conjunction with equipment to modernise some older trams on 1 November 1935. These cars were destined to become No 918-42. Again the bodies were built at Edge Lane. The first to appear, No 918, entered service on 5 September 1936. Deliveries continued contemporaneously with the first batch, with Nos 919-21 in September, Nos 922-26/28/29 in October, Nos 927/30-34 in November and Nos 935-40 in December. No 941 was new in October 1937 and the last, No 942, in November the same year. The last two cars inherited the Maley & Taunton trucks fitted to Nos 747/53 in 1936. Although this batch received the same GEC WT181AS motors as the earlier cars, there were a number of detail differences between the EMB and M&T bogies; the latter, for example, had a wheelbase of 4ft 6in making then 3in shorter than those supplied by EMB. The lighter bogies also meant that the cars weighed about a ton less overall than the EMB-fitted cars.

Before the appointment of Marks to the position of General Manager the post was temporarily vacant and the City Electrical Engineer, P. J. Robinson, was in charge of the undertaking. Under his aegis Liverpool gained a stylish batch of 36 cars, Nos 782-817 which became known as the 'Cabins'. The batch was built at Edge Lane between 1933 and 1935. No 795 is seen here when new in 1934. This particular car was ill-fated, being destroyed by fire in 1935 — an all too common a problem in Liverpool — and re-emerging in January 1936 in a form similar to that of the streamlined bogie cars. The 'Cabins' were the penultimate new trams to be built for the city before the appearance of the streamlined cars in 1936. *Real Photographs/IAL*

Simultaneously with the construction of the streamlined cars, Liverpool also had a programme for the modernisation of some of the 'Priestly' cars that were then between five and 10 years old. The plan was for 162 cars to be treated but, in the event, only 75 were completed. No 12, seen here at the Pier Head on 24 July 1949, was originally No 155 and was modernised in June 1938. The work included the fitting of a new truck, new motors, new brakes and reconditioned controllers.

Prior to the emergence of the Maley & Taunton-equipped cars, a further batch of 50, Nos 943-92, was authorised on 12 March 1936. The suppliers were to be the same as for the first batch. When new 12 were fitted with LW2 bogies — Nos 943-52/55/57 — whilst the remaining 38 received the 'Joburg'-type radial-arm bogies. All were fitted with GEC WT181AS motors, with the exception of Nos 963-92, which received four GEC WT184A motors, also rated at 40hp.

11 June 1936 was destined to be an important day for the type as the first three, Nos 868-70, entered service from Prince Alfred Road depot. The rest of the first batch followed over the succeeding months, with the last, No 917, appearing on 14 January 1937. A week later the first of the third batch, No 945, was completed and the last of this batch, No 992 (the highest numbered of any Liverpool tram), appeared on 27 June 1937.

The fourth, and final, batch of bogie cars was ordered on 10 November 1936. Again it was planned to build 50 cars (Nos 151-200), although in the event only the first 38 were completed. The construction of these cars required the renumbering of certain older cars. The equipment bought for the unfinished 12 (Nos 189-200) was used to re-equip certain older trams. The first of the batch entered service from Walton depot on 20 August 1937, at almost exactly the same time as the depot received the first of the streamlined four-wheel cars. The last bogie car, No 188, entered service on 17 December of the same year again at

The last non-streamlined trams acquired by Liverpool were the 50 bogie cars, Nos 818-67, produced in 1935-36 to a design of the new General Manager W. G. Marks. The cars owed much to the earlier work of Marks' predecessor, P. J. Robinson, but with detail differences. No 857, new in November 1935, is pictured at Pier Head on 24 July 1949.

Walton. Thirty-seven of this last batch were fitted with Lightweight bogies; the exception, No 181, was fitted with Heavyweight bogies. All received four GEC WT184A motors rated at 35hp and Metro-Vick control equipment.

Contemporary with the development of the bogie cars, work also proceeded with a four-wheel version — a type which became known as the 'Baby Grands'. The first mention of the need for a new four-wheel type occurred in October 1935 and tenders were invited at the end of 1936. Authorisation for a full batch of 100 was given on 12 April 1937 and the first, No 201, appeared on 26 November 1937. EMB won the contract for the trucks, of 9ft 0in wheelbase, whilst the motors for the first 13, Nos 201-13, were supplied by Metro-Vick (of the MV116AS type rated at 60hp), whilst the remainder (Nos 214-300) received motors supplied by BTH (of the 116AS type rated at 60hp). The new cars, similar in style to the bogie version, again had bodywork constructed at Edge Lane. The 'Baby Grands' were 33ft 10in long — three feet shorter than the bogie type — and could accommodate 70 seating passengers (30 in the lower saloon and 40 in the upper). The controllers for the new cars were salvaged from redundant 'Bellamy' cars and reconditioned before reuse.

Ten of the type were delivered in 1937; a further 77 in the following year. Twenty were delivered in 1939 and one in 1940 but the last two, Nos 299 and 300, were not delivered until 1942. No 300, which was delivered in October

No 925 was one of the Maley & Taunton-fitted batch of 'Green Goddesses' that were delivered in 1936. Seen here on 24 July 1949, this was one of 46 of the 'Green Goddesses' transferred to Glasgow in 1953-54. No 925 migrated to Scotland in January 1954; as No 1025 it was to survive until 1960.

Above:
'Baby Grand' No 258 was delivered in September 1938. It is pictured here at the terminus at Woolton on 24 July 1949. Note the buffer stops at the end of the running lines. No 258 was to survive in service until 1957, although the route No 4W to Woolton was not to survive this illustration long, being converted to bus operation on 15/16 October 1949.

Left:
No 983 was new in May 1937 and was fitted with EMB 'JB' bogies. Photographed at the Pier Head on 24 July 1949, the car shows clearly the lack of maintenance that was such a mark of Liverpool in the immediate postwar years. This particular car was one of several destroyed by fire at Walton depot on 1 March 1954.

of that year, was destined to be the last new tram delivered to Liverpool, but was, tragically, to have a life of only five years, being one of the many casualties of the Green Lane fire of 1947.

The war years were to be eventful in Liverpool since, as a major port, the city was high on the Luftwaffe's list of targets. Inevitably a number of Liverpool trams were damaged or destroyed by enemy action. The only streamlined car to be withdrawn as a direct consequence of the war was No 228, which was destroyed at Pier Head in July 1942. Other cars were damaged; for example, No 887 was out of service from October 1940 until 1944 due to bomb damage and No 166 was hit in 1942 but,

on this occasion, the car was quickly restored to service. No 228 was not, however, the only casualty during this period as a number of other cars were withdrawn as a result of fires and accidents: Nos 171 and 989 were destroyed by fire in Green Lane depot on 4 February 1942; No 209 was burnt out at Woolton in August 1945; No 217 was damaged by fire in April 1945, although not officially withdrawn until 1946; No 225 was destroyed by fire in April 1942; No 281 was withdrawn following fire damage in Bolton Street during July 1945; and No 943 was withdrawn in 1946, three years after overturning at Kirkby.

The propensity of the streamlined cars to burst into flames was one of the most severe faults of the type and one which was exacerbated by the declining standards of wartime maintenance. Water ingression, particularly around the destination blind area caused by an inherent weakness in the platform design, combined with poor cabling made for a potent and volatile combination. The fire at Green Lane depot, on 7 November 1947, destroyed a total of 30 streamlined cars ('Green Goddesses' Nos 159/63/73, 876/82/88/92/94-96/98, 908/12/15/59/60/80/82/87/91 and 'Baby Grands' Nos 233/34/56/82/90-92/94/95, 300) along with 36 other types. No 982 was not officially withdrawn until 1950 nor scrapped until 1955. The fire, which started on No 295, was to be one of the worst tramway fires in Britain. Fire was not the only problem to affect the streamlined cars; snow, too, could cause disruption through problems with the low-slung resistances. In both 1947 and 1950 heavy snowfalls led to the temporary withdrawal of the type, whilst the older cars continued to soldier on.

The Green Lane fire marked a watershed for the Liverpool system. Although, inevitably, the wartime years had seen little investment in new vehicles and routes, the policy of the Transport Department was still pro-tram and, indeed, Marks based his initial plans for the postwar city on the continued development of the tramway system. However, in October 1945, the Transport Committee voted for a policy of tramway conversion. This policy was confirmed by the full Council in November the same year. A full schedule for abandonment was developed by Marks and implementation of the scheme started in 1947. Although other operators offered Liverpool spare trams to replace the total of 66 destroyed at Green Lane, the city declined the offers, preferring to reduce the frequency on tram-operated services. Even before the fire Liverpool did not possess enough serviceable trams to operate a full service and buses had to provide support.

In the immediate postwar years the pressure was to restore the system to some semblance of order although, between 1945 and 1950, greater resources went into the bus operation. This exacerbated the already serious maintenance backlog from the war years and by 1950 there were some 100 modern trams out of service. Although a programme of reconstruction was instituted which saw all returned to service within two years, even as late as January 1952 No 868 could only effectively operate as a single-ended car. A total of 146 streamlined cars underwent major reconstruction between 1950 and 1953 and this led to certain alterations. For example, the half-drop windows were replaced with sliding windows and rewiring was also undertaken. A number of prefabricated end units were produced to enable accident-damaged cars to be repaired.

There were a number of modifications undertaken after 1945. The first of these was the result of an accident on 24 January 1945 when No 910 collided with No 850. This resulted in the withdrawal of No 910 and was one of a number of incidents attributable to the loss of air pressure. After an enquiry it was decided to fit Automatic Emergency Brakes and a buzzer to warn of low air pressure. This modification was slowly applied to all the streamlined cars. A number of cars received equipment salvaged from cars destroyed in the Green Lane fire: No 866 and 867 received Lightweight bogies and GEC WT184A motors, whilst Nos 879/881 and 957/92 also received replacement bogies.

During the post-1950 period a number of cars received replacement equipment: No 181 gained Heavyweight bogies; No 870 received Lightweight bogies and a rebuilt 'B' end (the latter from withdrawn No 988) in 1954; No 905 received four GEC WT181AS motors in 1952; No 955 received Heavyweight bogies (from No 965) in 1954; Nos 961/63/67 gained Lightweight bogies in 1954, as did No 982 at an unknown date.

The first closures in Liverpool's 10-year programme for tramway abandonment occurred in June 1948. Inevitably, the initial abandonments allowed for the balance between service and available fleet to be improved and, with the gradual improvement in the availability of the more modern cars, the older trams in the fleet were gradually withdrawn. A total of three routes were abandoned during 1948 and 14 the following year. Ten routes were converted during 1950 and nine in 1951. On 15 February 1951 No 990 carried the official last party for the closure of the routes to Bootle, when route No 35 (Seaforth-Fazakerley) was converted. The majority of routes to Bootle had been converted the previous November. The closures of 1950 and 1951 resulted in the 'Baby Grands' being housed at Green Lane and Edge Lane depots, whilst all the Maley & Taunton-fitted 'Green Goddesses' (Nos 918-42) were based at Garston. The remaining bogie cars were divided between Edge Lane, Walton and Green Lane depots.

A further eight routes were converted during 1952 and three the following year. The conversion of routes Nos 8 and 33 (both Pier Head-Garston) on 6 June 1953 resulted in the closure of Garston depot and the storage, pending sale to Glasgow, of the M&T batch of cars (with the exception of No 920 which was scrapped due to body defects). The last car at Garston depot was No 979 on 6 June. The full story of the 'Green Goddesses' in Scotland is narrated later.

By now the Liverpool system had been significantly reduced and the first withdrawals of streamlined cars from service for scrap occurred in September 1953 when six cars,

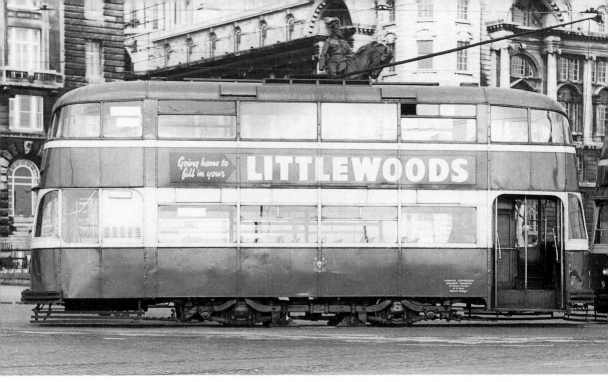

An interesting contrast in side views of the two types of Liverpool streamlined car; both views were taken at Pier Head in the mid-1950s. The upper of the two shows one of the 'Baby Grands' built in 1937-40 on EMB 9ft flexible axle trucks. These cars were slightly shorter than the 'Green Goddesses' and could accommodate 70 seated passengers.

The 'Green Goddesses' illustrated in the lower of the two photographs was 36ft 9in long and could seat a total of 78 passengers in the two saloons. This particular example was fitted with EMB Lightweight bogies. *Both Real Photographs/IAL*

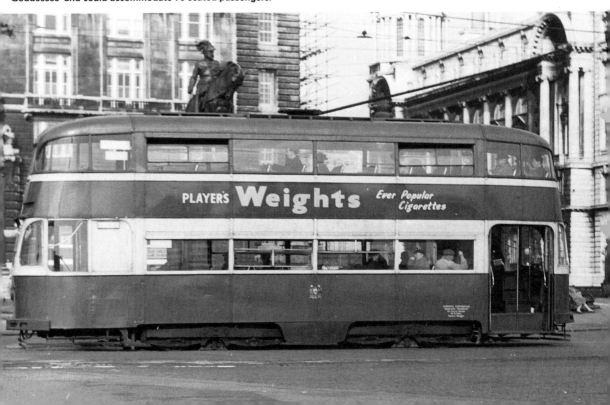

'Green Goddess' No 158 awaits departure from Liverpool Pier Head on route No 19 to Kirkby via Church Street. No 158 was one of a batch of 38 bogie cars delivered in 1937; although equipment was bought to complete a further 12, these were never built. All the batch, including No 156 were withdrawn by the end of 1956. Route No 19 was to disappear at the same time, being converted in November 1956. *Real Photographs/IAL*

including No 868 (the original car), were withdrawn and sold to Maden & Mackee. Apart from these withdrawals a number of other cars had also succumbed to the type's propensity to burst into flames. These included No 176 in October 1950, No 988 in 1953 and No 174 on 27 April 1954. In addition, there was also a further depot fire when, on 1 March 1954, three 'Green Goddesses' (Nos 965/83/85) were destroyed at Walton and a number of others damaged. A further fire, on 22 May 1955, saw No 964 destroyed at Walton Lane.

By mid 1955 the abandonment programme had resulted in the withdrawal of all the old cars and, with the sale to Glasgow, a total of 81 bogie cars and 84 four-wheelers remained in service. The policy was to withdraw the bogie cars in advance of the four-wheelers as the power consumption of the latter was lower than for the more powerful bogie cars. Following the conversion of five routes in 1954 and 1955, a total of eight services remained. The first casualties were routes Nos 13 (Pier Head-Lower Lane) and 14 (Pier Head-Utting Avenue East). As a result of these closures 35 cars were withdrawn — most ex-Walton 'Green Goddesses' — and in early 1956 46 bogie cars were sold to Maden & Mackee for scrap. This meant that the fleet was now reduced to 34 bogie cars and 84 'Baby Grands'. The bogie cars were allocated to Edge Lane and Walton, although they rarely appeared outside peak hours.

The next closures, on 3 November 1956, saw three routes converted — Nos 19 (Pier Head-Kirkby), 19A (Pier Head-Lower Lane) and 44 (Pier Head-Lower Lane). 'Baby Grand' No 206 was the last car from Kirkby and sister car No 207 the last from Southdene. No 293 was the last car on Scotland Road on route No 44. With the conversion of the Kirkby routes

Walton depot was closed and the remaining 31 bogie cars were withdrawn. Pending possible resale, the cars were transferred to Kirkby where No 153 was used as a mobile workmen's hut until 10 November when all the cars were moved to storage sidings on the industrial estate. Inevitably the hopes of selling the cars for further use proved forlorn and the cars were, therefore, sold to George Cohen for scrap. Dismantled at Kirkby, the last to disappear was No 186, which was scrapped on 26 April 1957.

There remained two operational routes, with 61 'Baby Grands' in service and another 11 in store. By early 1957 maintenance on the remaining fleet was reduced to the bare minimum with no further cars retyred after June and repainting (with the exception of No 293) ceasing. The 11 stored cars were sold for scrap in June 1957. The long drawn out closure process came to an end on 14 September 1957 when these last routes — Nos 6A (Pier Head-Bowring Park) and 40 (Castle Street-Page Moss Avenue) — were converted to bus operation. By the end only some 30 trams remained available for service and a total of 13 trams appeared in the closure procession (in order, Nos 210/64/14/35/13/26/76/60/96/52/45/07/93), with No 293 specially repainted in a reversed livery of cream with green bands as the official last car. After the closure all the cars passed to Edge Lane Works for disposal. The bulk had been pre-sold for scrap (the last, No 271, being dismantled in January 1958) although two were destined to survive: No 245 initially set aside for the BTC collection and No 293 for the Seashore Museum in the United States. The latter left its home town in May 1958, whilst the former has never moved away from the Merseyside area.

Thus, the story of the Liverpool streamlined cars in their home town came to an end, but this was not to be the end of the story so far as the bogie cars were concerned. The cars sold to Glasgow were still operational and to describe their history in Scotland it is necessary to retrace our steps back to the start of the decade.

In the early 1950s the city of Glasgow still had no definite plans for the conversion of the tramways system; indeed, the largest single batch of postwar trams — the 'Cunarders' — were still entering service and, whilst there had been odd conversions, most notably those connected with the introduction of trolleybuses, the system was largely intact. There remained, however, the problem that much of the fleet was formed of the 'Standard' cars built between 1899 and 1924 and urgently required replacement. If the prewar 'Coronation' programme had been completed, then the problem would not have existed to the same extent, but war had prevented the completion of the full 600 cars.

Although the system was not under threat, it is clear that there was not much enthusiasm for large scale investment in new tramcars and this led to the investigation of the second-hand market. Glasgow had examined both the Manchester 'Pilchers' and the London 'HR/2s' but had decided against both — the latter primarily due to the cost of installing improved braking. Thus, the contraction of the Liverpool system with the consequent availability of modern cars was to prove a godsend. On 13 May 1953 the Glasgow manager, E. R. L. Fitzpayne, reported to the Town Clerk that 20 bogie cars were available at £500 apiece (including the cost of transport). With an estimated cost of £100 to prepare them for service, this meant

that the cars would cost an average of £600 each. This was a considerable saving over the cost of buying or building new cars. The cars on offer were those fitted with Maley & Taunton swing link bogies and GEC WT184 motors, which had become non-standard in Liverpool. At 36ft 0in in length, the cars would be longer than the existing Glasgow fleet. This meant that the operation of the cars would be limited to around seven routes. Full agreement from the Corporation to proceed with the purchase was given on 11 June 1953.

The first car to be delivered to Glasgow, No 927 (which became No 1024), travelled northwards in September 1953 and this was followed in the same month by No 942 (No 1006). No 1006 was destined to become the first of the type to operate in Glasgow; No 927 was in poor condition — a reflection of the poor standards of maintenance in the postwar Liverpool — and was destined not to enter service until after No 1023 (Liverpool No 939), which was sent north in January 1954. Before entering service the cars were modified through the replacement of the trolleypole with Glasgow's normal bow collector (ironically a conversion that would probably have been carried out in Liverpool post-1945 if the tramway system had been retained), the fitting of replacement lifeguards and the removal of collision fenders in order to improve clearances. The bogies were also regauged from Liverpool's standard 4ft 8½in to Glasgow's unusual 4ft 7¾in. The cars were also repainted into the standard Glasgow livery of green, cream and orange. Clearance tests were carried out over much of the system, although the cars were ultimately allocated to Maryhill depot for use over the extended route No 29 (Tollcross-Milngavie [the service was extended from Ander-

To mark the closure of the Liverpool system, 'Baby Grand' No 293 was painted in a reverse livery and suitably inscribed. It is seen here in early September 1957 resplendent in its newly acquired livery. Following its role as the city's last car on 14 September No 293 was exported to the USA, where it remains to this day.
Liverpool Corporation

ston Cross to Milngavie on 4 October 1953]). The last of the first batch of cars, No 1030 (Liverpool No 919) entered service in April 1954. Although Parkhead received a small allocation of the cars, Maryhill depot was to be their primary home in Glasgow. The cars operated generally on routes Nos 15 (Anderston Cross-Baillieston) and 29.

In service the Glasgow cars suffered the same problems that had afflicted them in Liverpool. After a number of fires, the batch, starting with No 1008, were progressively rewired and other work was also undertaken. The Liverpool seats were replaced with traditional Glasgow seats, in order to improve working conditions for the conductors; whilst the problem of water ingression through the curved windows at the front end was partially solved through improved sealing. Despite the problems, Glasgow acquired a further 22 of the type in 1954; the first, No 878, heading north on 13 May 1954 and the last being No 875 which travelled in November of that year. By this stage the costs of bringing the cars up to Glasgow standards had increased to £1,250. The first of the second batch, Nos 1031 and 1032, entered service in September 1954. By December 1954, 19 of the second batch were still in store at Newlands depot, although only three remained by August 1955 and all had entered service by 1956.

Although these were the last cars to be acquired by Glasgow, the city retained an interest in the rest of Liverpool's modern fleet and, indeed, representatives of GCT visited the city on 25 March 1955 to examine the 'Baby Grands'. However, no purchase was pursued, nor were the remaining 'Goddesses' bought after withdrawal in late 1955.

Despite the investment in both new and second-hand cars, the Glasgow system was enter-

ing its final phase. No 1056 entered service in May 1956; it was destined to be the last tram to be placed in service by the city. Already, in November 1954, the Corporation had decided to replace 450 first-generation trams with buses and trolleybuses and in early 1955 Fitzpayne presented his proposals for the elimination of 10 routes and the withdrawal of 300 old cars. The remaining 150 old cars for withdrawal had already been partially replaced by this date through the acquisition of the Liverpool cars. The programme was agreed on 14 April 1955. A further policy shift saw the Corporation decide in early 1956 to abandon all routes outside the city boundary. It was, however, not until 1957 that total abandonment became a probability. On 24 June 1957 a report was submitted to the Transport Committee which examined the future costs of retaining the tramway system. The final decision to withdraw all the trams (over a 12-15-year period) was not, however, taken until 6 February 1958. In the event the time-scale was to be considerably shortened — the last trams operated barely four-and-a-half years later in September 1962.

That the tide was slowly turning against the tram became evident in August 1957 when No 1042 was involved in a serious accident. Whilst earlier accident victims had been speedily repaired, the costs involved in repairing No 1042 were considered prohibitive and the car was withdrawn. As non-standard cars in terms both of operational availability and construction, the 'Green Goddesses' were to be relatively early casualties amongst the modern cars. By the end of 1959 only seven of the type remained in service — Nos 1012/16/25/32/33/36/55 — and even these were to be withdrawn shortly afterwards. Four were withdrawn in March 1960 (Nos 1012/16/25/33) and one —

No 1032 — in April. The withdrawal of No 1055 in June left only one, No 1036, in service and this was withdrawn in July. Route No 29, upon which the ex-Liverpool cars had generally operated, was to outlast the type by some four months, being converted to bus operation in November 1960.

Of the 46 cars that travelled north, only one, No 1055 (Liverpool No 869), was to survive.

'Green Goddess' No 1015 heads eastbound through the Glaswegian rain *en route* to Tollcross on route No 29. No 1015 was originally Liverpool No 940 and dated from December 1936. Withdrawn in 1953, it entered service in Glasgow in December of that year, being withdrawn finally in June 1959. *W. J. Haynes*

Acquired for preservation, it was stored for a short period at Middleton, where it suffered slight vandalism, before moving to Crich on 26 November 1961. It temporarily left Crich for restoration in its home town on 12 February 1967. In Liverpool it was stored at Green Lane depot. Although it returned to the museum fully restored it has yet to be operated at the museum and, at the time of writing, is undergoing a further major restoration with the intention that it will operate again. When it does so, No 869 will become the first Liverpool tram to operate in Britain for more than 30 years. It will be the most expensive restoration undertaken at Crich and the newly completed car is scheduled to re-enter service on 24 July 1993.

Green Goddesses — Liverpool-Glasgow

	In service	To Glasgow	Glasgow Number	In service	Withdrawn
869	June 1936	April 1954	1055	November 1955	June 1960*
871	June 1936	August 1954	1047	August 1955	March 1959
874	June 1936	September 1954	1044	July 1955	February 1959
875	June 1936	November 1954	1046	July 1955	October 1958
877	June 1936	September 1954	1045	July 1955	October 1959
878	July 1936	May 1954	1041	June 1955	April 1959
880	July 1936	September 1954	1037	May 1955	March 1959
881	July 1936	August 1954	1033	January 1955	March 1960
883	July 1936	August 1954	1038	May 1955	June 1959
884	July 1936	June 1954	1053	September 1955	July 1959
885	July 1936	June 1954	1034	April 1955	February 1959
886	August 1936	August 1954	1042	June 1955	August 1957
887	August 1936	October 1954	1048	August 1955	October 1959
890	August 1936	May 1954	1054	October 1955	August 1959
891	August 1936	June 1954	1036	May 1955	July 1960
893	September 1936	September 1954	1049	August 1955	June 1959
897	October 1936	October 1954	1052	September 1955	December 1959
899	October 1936	June 1954	1031	September 1954	February 1960
901	October 1936	July 1954	1032	December 1954	April 1960
902	October 1936	July 1954	1035	May 1955	July 1959
903	November 1936	October 1954	1043	June 1955	March 1959
904	November 1936	October 1954	1056	May 1956	November 1959
918	September 1936	January 1954	1022	February 1953	May 1959
919	September 1936	March 1954	1030	April 1954	February 1960
921	September 1936	November 1953	1016	December 1953	March 1960
922	October 1936	December 1953	1018	December 1953	May 1959
923	October 1936	October 1953	1012	November 1953	March 1960
924	October 1936	February 1954	1027	March 1954	August 1959
925	October 1936	January 1954	1025	February 1954	March 1960
926	October 1936	December 1953	1019	January 1954	November 1959
927	November 1936	September 1953	1024	February 1954	June 1958
928	October 1936	November 1953	1013	December 1953	March 1959
929	October 1936	March 1954	1029	April 1954	May 1959
930	November 1936	October 1953	1010	November 1953	June 1959
931	November 1936	October 1953	1011	November 1953	February 1959
932	November 1936	November 1953	1014	December 1953	October 1959
933	November 1936	February 1954	1028	March 1954	January 1959
934	November 1936	September 1953	1007	October 1953	September 1959
935	December 1936	October 1953	1009	November 1953	April 1959
936	December 1936	December 1953	1021	January 1954	February 1960
937	December 1936	December 1953	1020	January 1954	October 1958
938	December 1936	October 1953	1008	October 1953	February 1959
939	December 1936	January 1954	1023	February 1954	August 1959
940	December 1936	November 1953	1015	December 1953	June 1959
941	October 1937	February 1954	1026	March 1954	September 1959
942	November 1937	September 1953	1006	October 1953	October 1959

Notes:
* No 1055 (No 869) preserved after withdrawal. Currently operating at the National Tramway Museum.
There was no No 1017 as that number was filled by one of the ex-Paisley cars cut-down to single-deck for use as a driver training vehicle.

9

The LCC 'HR/2s'

The tramway system of the London County Council was by far the largest in England. Its complex network of lines stretched widely throughout the Metropolis, reaching as far east as Abbey Wood and Forest Gate, as far south as Grove Park, Streatham and Tooting, as far west as Shepherds Bush and Hammersmith and as far north as Stamford Hill and Highgate. In serving the core of London, the LCC system provided links (albeit not always physical) with the rest of London's tramway operators, both municipal and company owned. The LCC could also lay claim to the unique Kingsway Subway — Britain's only tram subway.

To operate this immense network of lines, the LCC possessed, at 1 July 1933 when its operations were taken over by the newly-formed LPTB, more than 1,600 electric trams, making it by far the biggest single fleet in the British Isles. Of this fleet some 1,000 were of the 'E/1' type, built between 1907 and 1922. The remaining cars were divided into a number of smaller classes, including the 'E/3s', which numbered around 100, and the 'HR/2s', which totalled 109 in all.

Amongst the LCC's network of routes were a number serving Dog Kennel Hill between Camberwell and Dulwich. These routes were served by cars from Camberwell depot. Operation over this steeply graded 380yd section was heavily

restricted by the Board of Trade, which decreed that, in order to avoid accidents from runaway trams, only one car at a time was permitted to occupy either the up or down track. In order to circumvent the restriction, the LCC gained powers in 1911 to lay an additional pair of tracks, giving two uphill and two downhill lines for operation.

The origin of the 'HR/2s' — the 'HR' stood for 'Hilly Route' — can be dated to the construction of two prototype cars in 1929. The first, designated 'HR/1', was No 1852. This car was built by the LCC at Charlton Works on EMB equal-wheel trucks with roller bearing axles. All four axles were motored — four Metro-Vick MV109 motors rated at 35hp each — and the car was fitted with Metro-Vick OK29B controllers. The body was similar in design to the 'E/1s' then being constructed. The track brakes were arranged in such a way as to allow a partial application before descending steep hills. The seating capacity was 46 in the upper saloon and 28 in the lower. The car passed to

With over 1,000 cars constructed between 1907 and 1930, the LCC 'E/1' cars were both the mainstay of the system and also the single largest class of tram built for a British tramway. No 1142, seen here operating on route No 16 towards Croydon prior to the creation of the LPTB in 1933, was one of batch built by Hurst Nelson and delivered in 1908-9. Some 154 of the type, albeit not No 1142, were rehabilitated during the late 1930s. Whilst many of the older cars were withdrawn during the trolleybus conversion programme, many others were to survive until the final demise of London's trams in 1950-52. *W. J. Haynes*

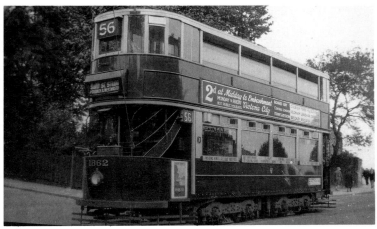

Although delivered in 1930 'HR/2' No 1862 was constructed, as were the majority of London County Council cars, with open platforms. This somewhat archaic design was the result of Metropolitan Police restrictions. Seen in its LCC livery No 1862 would later be fitted with enclosed windscreens. As with the majority of the class, No 1862 was to survive until 'Operation Tramaway'.
W. J. Haynes

Left:
Developed alongside the 'HR/2s', the 'E/3s', which were produced for both the LCC and Leyton Corporation, were designed to replace the LCC's fleet of old 'A' and 'D' type cars. The LCC cars were a combination of Hurst Nelson bodies and EMB maximum-traction bogies. As with the 'HR/2s', existing regulations meant that the 'E/3s' had to be delivered with open lower-deck vestibules, as shown on this pre-1933 shot of No 1905 heading towards Savoy Street on route No 40. As the cars were designed for use on Kingsway Subway routes, an illuminated sign 'via Kingsway Subway' was displayed above the destination blind. When not operating on such a route, as on this occasion, the illuminated display could be blanked out.
W. J. Haynes

the LPTB in 1933 but was one of 29 casualties when, on 8 September 1940, Camberwell depot was destroyed during the blitz.

The second experimental car was the first 'HR/2', No 1853. In terms of electrical equipment and trucks No 1853 was very similar to its predecessor. The major change came with the body. Again built by the LCC at Charlton, No 1853 was graced by an all-metal body (lower deck in steel and the upper in aluminium) of a new design. Although the seating capacity was the same as No 1852, the changed body style provided more internal space. Half-drop windows provided fresh air for the upper deck, whilst the lower saloon was given mechanically operated vents. No 1853 was a further casualty of the destruction of Camberwell depot on 8 September 1940.

The second batch of 'HR/2s', Nos 101-59 was largely constructed for service over the Highgate Hill section in North London. As this batch's operational area was conduit-equipped throughout the cars were not fitted with trolleypoles. No 141 is seen awaiting departure from the Moorgate terminus of route No 11 to Highgate Village, a service which was converted to bus operation in 1938.
D. Sutton/IAL

The 'HR/2s' were constructed with all-metal bodies so that they could operate through the modernised Kingsway Subway. No 132, one of the conduit-only cars, is seen entering the southern portal of the subway *en route* to Highgate on route No 35. *D. Sutton/IAL*

There were two production batches of 'HR/2s'. The first were Nos 1854-1903, which were authorised on 17 March 1929 and built in 1930 by English Electric on EMB heavy duty equal-wheel trucks (of Type 6). The cost of the trucks amounted to some £15,600. These were based at Camberwell (although some did see service from New Cross in this period) and replaced the older 'C' and 'M' class cars. This batch was fitted with both plough and two trolley poles. As with the preproduction cars, this batch was equipped with Metro-Vick MV109 motors (of 35hp) and OK29B controllers. The all-metal bodies for the cars ensured that no part of the LCC system (including the Kingsway Subway once altered to allow the running of double-deck cars) was barred; in practice, however, the cars rarely operated away from the Dog Kennel Hill routes. In accordance with the existing Metropolitan Police restrictions, these cars were delivered with open lower deck platforms, which offered the driver no protection. Full wooden-framed windscreens were eventually fitted to all the class. The average cost of the cars was a total of £3,540.

On 3 September 1930 one of the first batch of cars was tested over the Highgate Hill route in north London. This led, later in the same month, to a request for a further batch of cars to operate over this route. Authorisation was given for the purchase of 60 cars. The second batch, Nos 101-59, was built by Hurst Nelson in 1931 on EMB radial arm equal-wheel bogies (of Type 6a). Metro-Vick MV109Z motors (of 35hp) and OK37B controllers were fitted. These cars were provided with metal-framed lower deck windscreens from new. Unlike the earlier batch, these cars were fitted for conduit operation only. The second batch differed in detail from the first. The final car of this order, No 160, was built originally as an 'HR/2' but its trucks and

electrical equipment were used under the experimental car No 1. In place, No 160 gained EMB bogies of Type 4a, two English Electric DK126A motors (rated at 57.5hp) and English Electric CDB2 controllers. This car became classified 'E/3'. Whilst intended primarily for the Highgate Hill route (and based, therefore, at Holloway) a number of this batch of 'HR/2s' were also allocated to Camberwell for use on the Dog Kennel Hill routes. The average cost per car of this batch was £2,884.

In terms of dimensions, the 'HR/2s' were 33ft 10in long and provided seating for 46 in the upper saloon and 28 in the lower. Additional braking capacity, in the form of electric runback brakes, was fitted as were more normal hand-wheel and magnetic track brakes. Although relatively new, four of the 'HR/2s' were involved in the 'Rehabilitation' programme during the mid-1930s. The first to appear was No 1885 in November 1936, with three others, Nos 1884/87/90, appearing during the following month.

In December 1939 the tram route serving Highgate Hill — No 11 from Moorgate to Highgate Village — was converted to trolleybus operation as part of the LPTB's prewar trolleybus conversion scheme. The remaining 'HR/2s' allocated to Hampstead were, consequently, sent south of the river.

During 1939 three of the class, Nos 1881/83/86, were sold to Leeds and, if war had not intervened, it is likely that more of the class would have migrated northwards as the gradual conversion of the LPTB system to trol-

leybus operation started to affect the ex-LCC routes. In the event, these were the only three to be operated outside London.

Inevitably, there were a significant number of losses during the war, particularly given the destruction of Camberwell depot. Eight of the first batch (Nos 1865/89/98-903) and eight of the second (Nos 112/23-25/29-31/48) were destroyed and others were damaged. Two of those most severely damaged, Nos 127 (in 1941) and 1893 (in 1942), were heavily rebuilt; the former gaining an ex-'E/1' upper deck to replace its own destroyed one.

As with the rest of the remaining London system, the pressure after the cessation of hostilities in 1945 was not the immediate abandonment of the trams, but the restoration of a decent standard of service. The ultimate intention to abandon the trams in favour of buses was confirmed in November 1946, prior to the establishment of the London Transport Executive in 1948, but it was not to be until 1950 that the conversion programme — codenamed 'Operation Tramaway' — was to start.

At the start of the conversion programme all the 'HR/2s' which had survived World War 2 remained in service. A total of 90 remained based at Camberwell and the first withdrawals were not to occur for almost a year. The first

Seen on a Southern Counties Tourist Society trip on 9 May 1948, No 1885 passes through Bloomsbury. One of four 'HR/2s' to be rehabilitated during the late 1930s, No 1885 was to survive until Stage 7 of 'Operation Tramaway', in April 1952, when 18 of the type were to be withdrawn. *V. C. Jones/IAL*

casualty was No 1895, which was withdrawn in the late summer of 1951, between Stages 4 and 5 of 'Operation Tramaway'. The conversion programme was soon to affect the 'HR/2s', however, as Stage 5 (6-7 October 1951) was to see trams withdrawn from the Dog Kennel Hill routes (such as routes Nos 56/84 from Embankment to Peckham Rye, 60 Dulwich Library to Southwark, 62, Lewisham-Savoy Street and 58 Blackwall Tunnel-Victoria). This stage was to see 98 trams withdrawn, of which many were to be the conduit-only batch of 'HR/2s'. Withdrawn at this time were Nos 105-11/13-17/19/20/26-28/36/37/41-44/47/49-53/56/58 which were all despatched for scrap at the Penhall Road 'Tramatorium'. A further four (Nos 101-4) were stored at Penhall Road, but they were never to re-enter service. Following the conversion of these routes, a number of the trolleypole-fitted 'HR/2s' were transferred to New Cross depot.

The next stage of 'Operation Tramaway', No 6, on 5-6 January 1952 saw a further six day time and one all-night service converted. More than 100 trams were withdrawn, including more of the 1931 batch of 'HR/2s' — Nos 133-35/38-40/45/46/54/57/59. The other four cars of this batch, Nos 118/21/22/32, were also withdrawn at this time, but were reinstated. Between Stages 6 and 7 No 1879 was withdrawn following an accident. The four reprieved cars were finally to succumb during Stage 7 on 5-6 April 1952. Also withdrawn at this time were a number of the trolleypole-fitted batch — Nos 1878/80/82/84/85/87/88/90-94/96/97. Between Stages 7 and 8 (the last) six more of the type were withdrawn — Nos 1860/66/68/70/74/76. This meant that there remained only 17 of the type in service by 'Last Tram Week'. The final rites of the London system were played out on the weekend of 5-6 July 1952 as the Metropolis bade farewell to the tram. A number of 'HR/2s' were in service on the last day, including No 1861 on route No 72 which ran with the chalk legend 'GOING CHEAP COMPLETE WITH TEA CAN'. In fact, the only place that these cars were going — with one exception — was to the 'Tramatorium', where they were broken up in the following months. Ten sets of equipment were salvaged, however, and exported to Egypt. The one

exception was No 1858, which was sold to Peter J. Davis.

Having seen the fate of the 'HR/2s' in London, it is now necessary to retrace our steps slightly and examine the history of those cars which were sold in 1939. With the gradual elimination of the London network, three of the 'HR/2s' were sold to Leeds. These were Nos 1881/83/86, which became Nos 277-79 respectively in Leeds. The first of the three entered service in Yorkshire in October 1939, the second in December 1939 and the last in June 1940. Whilst there were tentative plans for Leeds to acquire further examples, the onset of war and the consequent delay to the tramway conversion programme in the Metropolis meant that these plans were thwarted.

Although the 1854-1903 batch of 'HR/2s' were normally fitted with EMB radial trucks of Type 6, the three cars supplied to Leeds had trucks of Type 6A, which were normally to be found under the 101-59 batch of cars. It seems probable that the bogies were transferred in London — certainly Nos 108/12/15 later ran with incorrect Type 6 bogies — and No 1898 also operated in London with the Type 6A bogies.

In Leeds little was done to alter the cars initially, although bow collectors were fitted and the trio were painted in the Leeds livery of pale blue. However, the standard of service was considered poor compared to existing Leeds cars, and the 'HR/2s' soon found themselves relegated to the short Hunslet route. In order to improve the cars, modifications were undertaken. No 277 was the first to be treated with the installation of platform air doors, and Maley

& Taunton air wheel and track brakes. The car re-entered service on 26 June 1943. From this date on until eventual withdrawal the car was to operate generally over the routes to Roundhay, Moortown and Lawnswood.

In 1946 No 279 was temporarily taken out of service. Its bogies were used in the construction of a demonstration mock-up vehicle. Given that at this date Leeds was actively pursuing a tram subway policy, it is possible that this mock-up was a single-deck car. In any event, the 'HR/2' returned to service in June of that year.

No 277 was further modified in 1948 with an alteration to the bell-push arrangement — a modification also undertaken on most of the post-1930 cars in the fleet — and the use of pale blue moquette on the lower saloon seats, after which the car emerged in a new variation of the pale blue livery. This livery featured the first use of Gill Sans fleet numbers in place of the earlier variety. The three 'HR/2s' were classified 'F1' when the system was introduced in Leeds in 1948.

Although the cars were normally limited to specific routes — Hunslet and later those to Lawnswood, Roundhay and Moortown — they were seen elsewhere on occasion. For example, on 21 August 1949 No 278 was used on an LRTL tour, which took the car to the Stanningley and New Inn routes for the first time.

In early 1951 No 278 was modified through the introduction of platform doors, Maley & Taunton air brakes and single destination indicators. The fitting of air brakes was a result of renewed interest from Leeds (and also from Glasgow) in the remaining 'HR/2s'; the Ministry of Transport would not permit the sale and

Below:
No 133, one of 59 'HR/2s' built by Hurst Nelson in 1930, is seen in Peckham Rye on 25 June 1950. Route No 56, from Peckham Rye to Embankment (via Westminster) was to be converted to bus operation in October 1951, whilst No 133 was not to last much longer, being withdrawn in January 1952. *V. C. Jones/IAL*

Above right:
The change-pit was one of the characteristic features of the London tramway system. Here, pictured on a Southern Counties Touring Society special, No 1877 is seen at the change-pit at Downham Way. No 1877 was one of a number of 'HR/2s' to survive until the final closure of the London system in July 1952. *V. C. Jones/IAL*

Below right:
The first of the three Leeds 'HR/2s', No 277, is pictured at Middleton terminus during an LRTL tour on 23 October 1948. Originally No 1881 in the London County Council fleet, the car had been sold to Leeds in 1939. The three 'HR/2s' were designated Class F1 in Leeds during 1948. No 277 was to last in service until 1957 and was scrapped during September that year. At this stage Middleton remained a terminus, but the following year was to see one of the few postwar tram extensions built in Britain when the line from Middleton to Belle Isle was completed.

operation of the cars outside London without the fitting of air brakes. The experimental conversion of No 278 proved that the exercise was costly and the proposed transfer did not take place. The completion of No 278 saw the car painted in an experimental vermilion livery — one of four cars so treated — at a time when Leeds was testing a variety of alternative liveries to replace the existing blue. Following modification of the airbrake in 1952 to the UCC type No 278 was allocated to Chapeltown depot.

In 1953 No 279 was repainted into the new red livery and was fitted with single blind destination indicators. This was the last of the trio to remain in blue livery. It was not fitted with air brakes and was consequently normally used only on the Hunslet route. By the mid-1950s the gradual conversion of the Leeds system meant that non-standard types were increasingly under threat. In June 1957 it was reported that 41 cars, including the three 'HR/2s', were available for disposal. The trio was actually withdrawn on 29 September 1957 with the conversion of the Moortown-Dewsbury Road route. All three were scrapped.

Leeds 'HR/2' No 279 is seen at the terminus of route No 25 in Hunslet. It is pictured in the pale blue livery which it was to retain until 1953. The car's destination display was also to be modified in 1953, when a single blind replaced the arrangement illustrated here. The Hunslet route was the regular haunt of No 279 as it remained unfitted with air brakes. Until abandonment in the early 1930s it was possible to travel beyond Hunslet by tram to Rothwell and Wakefield with through services operated by West Riding.
W. J. Haynes

With the demise of the three survivors in Leeds, this meant that the only 'HR/2' to survive was No 1858. Since 2 October 1952 this car had been displayed at Chessington Zoo in Surrey — on a site previously occupied by a bison! — but, being in the open, the ravages of the British weather were leading to a deterioration in its condition. The car was transferred to the East Anglian Transport Museum at Carlton Colville on 7-8 April 1964. Now operational again, No 1858 gives a new generation the opportunity to ride on an 'HR/2'.

10

The 'Felthams'

Whilst much of the London tramway system was controlled by the London County Council, or by municipal operators, there were also a number of significant company-owned systems. Of these, the two most important were London United Tramways, with a network centred around Kingston, and Metropolitan Electric Tramways, which operated to the north and west of the Metropolis. By the mid-1920s both of these companies were faced by the need to re-equip and the result was, eventually, the dramatic 'Feltham' class.

Both LUT and MET were ultimately controlled by the 'UndergrounD' group, a group which also had interests in the growing network of underground railways in London and which also controlled the Union Construction Co Ltd. This company, which had been registered as early as 1901, was, however, not to undertake an active role until much later in the group's activities. The almost moribund company was revitalised in the mid-1920s for, at first, the refurbishment of rolling stock for the Central line and later for the construction of tube trains for the Piccadilly and Bakerloo lines. This work was all carried out at the company's premises at Feltham — two old aircraft hangars.

Under the aegis of the company's General Manager, C. J. Spencer, a number of experimental trams had been built from 1926 onwards. The first of these, MET No 318, emerged in 1927. Painted in a light blue and cream livery, the car was nicknamed 'Bluebell'. Built at MET's works at Hendon on Brush maximum traction bogies, No 318 provided seats for 71 passengers. It entered service on 10 March 1927 and operated largely between Finchley and Cricklewood. (No 318 was rebuilt on several occasions and was involved in a serious accident in 1928. Following the accident, the car was repaired and repainted in the standard MET livery of red and cream. It became No 2255 in 1933 and was withdrawn for scrap in August 1936.)

The second experimental car was allocated the stock No 139 (believed to be an error and that No 319 was its intended number) and was built by London General at Chiswick on Brush Mountain & Gibson-type maximum traction trucks. On completion the car was transferred to LUT, where it became No 350, and operated on route No 57 from Hounslow to Shepherds Bush. Nicknamed 'Poppy', the car became No 2317 in the 1933 renumbering. Latterly operating with replacement trucks, the car was withdrawn following the conversion of route No 57 to trolleybus operation on 27 October 1935.

With the experience derived from the two experimental cars, it now proved possible to involve UCC in the modernisation programme. Three trial cars were to be the result: MET No 320, which emerged in April 1929; No 330 in October 1929; and, finally, No 331 in June 1930.

No 320 was the first tramcar to be built by UCC and its design was far in advance of its time. The body frame was constructed of steel, with aluminium panelling, except for the dashes, which were of steel. The driving cabs, designed to enable the driver to sit, projected from the front of the lower deck saloons. The equal-wheel trucks were manufactured by MET at Hendon and four Metro-Vick MV101 motors, rated at 35hp each, were fitted. The controllers were of the English Electric DB2 type. With passenger flow in mind, the car also incorporated front exits. No 320 was allocated to Finchley depot and operated on route No 40, from Whetstone to Cricklewood. It was destined to last in service only until the conversion of route

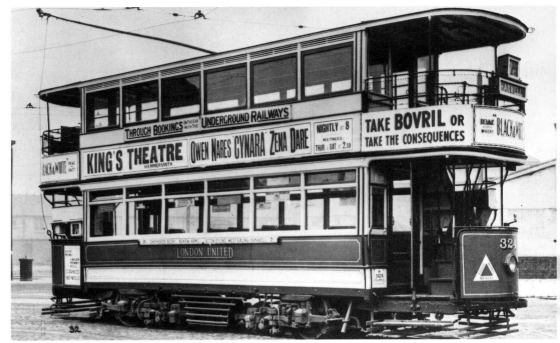

Above and left:
Prior to the development of the 'Felthams' both LUT and MET undertook modernisation of their existing fleets. LUT No 324 was one of a batch of 40 cars built by UEC in 1906. These were modernised in 1925-28 by the fitting of replacement motors and controllers. All 40 passed to the LPTB but were quickly to succumb to the trolleybus conversion programme and all were withdrawn by the end of 1936. MET No 314 was one of the company's 'H' class cars which were introduced in 1910 and were built by either Brush or by MET itself. All were modernised in 1928-29 through the fitting (with one exception) of new motors and altered seating. No 314 was to become LPTB No 2246 and was withdrawn in 1938. *Real Photographs/IAL*

No 40 to trolleybus operation in 1936 having been renumbered 2166 in 1933.

The second car, No 330, again had trucks produced at Hendon. This time, however, they were maximum traction fitted with two BTH 509 motors, rated at 60hp each. The controllers were BTH B527As, which were originally designed to control four motors and which, therefore, had to be modified for use with the two BTH 509s. Structurally very similar to No 320, No 330's most significant change was that it was designed for Pay As You Enter operation, with a conductor and ticket machine placed near the entrance. Also allocated to route No 40, experience showed that the scheme was not successful and normal methods of fare collection were soon adopted. The car became No 2167 in 1933 and was destined to be transferred south with the conversion of

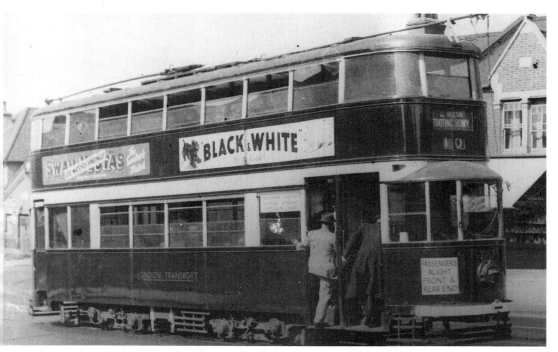

the ex-MET routes in the mid-1930s. It was finally withdrawn in 1949 and scrapped at Purley depot.

The third, and final, experimental car was No 331. The car received the equal-wheel trucks built at Hendon that had been originally intended for No 330 and also received four GEC WT18 motors, rated at 35hp each and BTH B49 controllers. The seating capacity was 28 in the lower saloon and 48 in the upper. The body was fitted with centre entrances — the only MET car so designed and selected for the possible use of PAYE operation — with air-operated doors. The driver's cabs were raised so that normal controllers could be used whilst allowing the seated driver the same line of vision as he would have had standing in a normal tram. The car became No 2168 in 1933 and was withdrawn in 1936; stored for a period, it was sold to Sunderland (where it became No 100) for £250 in January 1937. Transport north cost an additional £548. The car operated in Sunderland largely on the Durham Road route until final withdrawal in 1953. Preserved on withdrawal, No 331 is now displayed at the National Tramway Museum.

Contemporaneously with the development of the experimental cars by UCC — the company changed its name to the Union Construction & Finance Co Ltd in February 1929 — the MET was involved in negotiations regarding the renewal of the lease of its routes from Middle-

sex County Council. As part of their agreement for renewing the lease, the County Council requested the replacement of old rolling stock and in July 1929 Frank Pick (a director of MET) told the council that if the leases were renewed that new cars would be ordered. The formal approval for the order of 100 new trams was given on 3 April 1930. Of the 100, 54 (excluding No 331 already under construction) would be for MET (Nos 319/21-29/32-75) and the remaining 46 for LUT (Nos 351-96). The order was announced officially in August 1930 and deliveries were scheduled to begin in December of the same year.

The bodies were constructed at Feltham. They were built of welded steel framing with mild steel panelling on the lower decks and aluminium on the upper, with the twin staircases forming an integral part of the framework. The driver's cabs were raised in a similar fashion to those on No 331. Initially, the cars were built

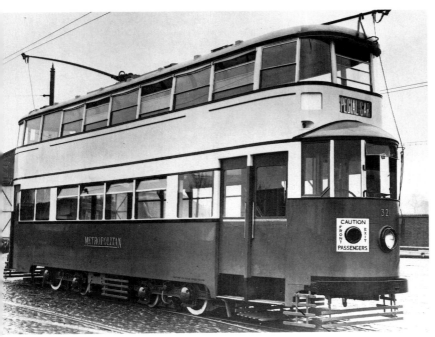

MET No 321 was the second of the company's production batch of 'Felthams'. It is seen here when brand new. Points to note include the lack of full windscreen — in order to fulfil the existing regulations and which required the driver to wear protective clothing during bad weather — and the warning to following traffic that the car was front exit. This car became LPTB No 2067 in 1933 and was one of six of the type scrapped between 1947 and 1949 as the result of accident damage. *Real Photographs/IAL*

with a gap beneath the windscreens — requiring the drivers to wear waterproof aprons — to fulfil the existing regulations. These were, however, soon amended and the gaps removed. The bodies were also designed with front exits. After the completion of the work at Feltham, the unpainted bodies were transported to the Fulwell depot of LUT where the trucks and electrical equipment were fitted.

For cost reasons, it had been decided to utilise only two motors and therefore maximum traction trucks of a 4ft 6in wheelbase, supplied by EMB, were used. The MET cars were fitted with BTH 509P1 motors, rated at 60hp, and OK33B controllers. The LUT cars were fitted with GEC WT29 motors, rated at 60hp, and GEC KB5 controllers. The length of the cars meant that twin trolley poles were fitted and, for the MET batch, provision was also made for the conduit plough. The ex-LUT cars were so converted when they were transferred south of the

river in the late 1930s. One exception was LUT No 396 which received English Electric equalwheel trucks (which utilised cardan shaft drive), DK131 motors and CBD2 controllers. The nonstandard equipment in No 396 was replaced in 1937, probably by the trucks from the nowwithdrawn No 2317 *Poppy*. Although officially designated Class UCC, the trams became widely known as the 'Felthams'.

Initially there was confusion with the front exits, and this led to the development of 'STOP' signals, which warned following traffic and which were first tested on No 329 in July 1931. With the success of the trial, the modification was made to the full fleet.

London United 'Feltham' No 396 is seen outside Fulwell depot when new. No 396 was the last of LUT's 46 'Felthams' and became LPTB No 2165 in 1933. In 1937 the trucks and electrical equipment on this car were replaced by equipment salvaged from No 2317. The car later received BTH B49 controllers. Withdrawn following accident damage in the late 1940s, this was one of the few 'Felthams' not to migrate north to Leeds. Another LUT depot, Hanwell, was home to all the LUT 'Felthams' before the conversion programme led to their transfer south of the river. *Charles F. Klapper/Courtesy of the Omnibus Society and A. D. Packer*

Left:
After withdrawal by the LPTB in 1936, No 2168 (MET No 331) was sold to Sunderland in January 1937 becoming No 100 — the highest numbered tram — in the fleet. It was destined to survive on Wearside until withdrawal in March 1952. Rescued for preservation, it led a nomadic existence — including a spell in Bradford City Transport's workshops at Thornbury — before arriving at Crich. It is seen here at Seaburn in May 1950.

Below left:
Ex-MET 'Feltham' No 2070 trundles through Streatham on 15 July 1949. No 2070 was one of six 'Felthams' to be withdrawn in August 1950, before the commencement of 'Operation Tramaway', and was amongst the first sent to Leeds. Becoming No 507 in the Leeds fleet, the car was destined for a relatively short life, being withdrawn after an accident on 4 September 1952 and scrapped in August 1955.

Apart from the cost of the actual vehicles, which came to a total of just over £3,500 per car for MET, there was also a considerable amount of work undertaken to accommodate these much longer cars. In June 1930, for example, MET had authorised the expenditure of £198,000 for depot work at Finchley and other track work, such as the lengthening of the siding at Edmonton town hall.

The first MET 'Felthams' entered service on 1 February 1931 on route No 40. The MET cars were initially allocated to Finchley depot and as later cars were delivered so the first delivered were transferred to Wood Green. Apart from route No 40, the 'Felthams' also operated over

the joint route No 21, North Finchley-Holborn, and No 29, Enfield-Tottenham Court Road, in conjunction with LCC cars. The 'Felthams' were barred from Barnet after tests found insufficient clearance at the foot of Barnet Hill. The last MET 'Feltham' was delivered on 29 October 1931.

The first LUT cars were delivered to Hanwell depot and eight entered service on route No 7 from Uxbridge to Shepherds Bush. It had been proposed in late 1929 that this route would have been reconstructed partly on reserved sleeper track; in the event the work was not undertaken, and this meant that the potential of the cars was not properly exploited. The LUT 'Felthams' also possibly saw service on route No 55 from Brentford to Hanwell. There is no photographic evidence for this although Hanwell depot was enlarged for use by the 'Felthams'.

The pattern was set now for the period up until the creation of the London Passenger Transport Board on 1 July 1933. Under London Transport, the ex-MET cars were numbered

Telford Avenue depot was home to the 'Felthams' during their last years in London. No 2093 is pictured outside the depot on 16 January 1949. The tram was destined to be withdrawn as a result of Stage 1 of 'Operation Tramaway' on 30 September 1950. It became No 515 in the Leeds fleet and was eventually one of 17 'Felthams' to remain operational until closure in November 1959.

2066-119 in sequence and the ex-LUT examples became Nos 2120-65. However, even
before the creation of the LPTB, moves were
afoot that would dramatically change the transport of west and north London. The London
United Tramways Act of August 1930 empow-
ered the company to operate trolleybuses over
the bulk of its system and work started soon
after on erecting overhead between Twicken-
ham and Teddington. The new trolleybus services were inaugurated on 16 May 1931.
Although there were significant numbers of
new trams in London when the LPTB was cre-
ated, it soon became clear that the Board envisaged the conversion of much of the system to
trolleybus operation.

Powers were soon obtained for the policy
and on 27 October 1935 route No 57 was converted to trolleybus operation. This was followed on 2 August 1936 when route No 45 (the
former MET route No 40) was similarly treated.
This led to the transfer of a number of the
'Felthams' from Finchley to Wood Green. The
increase in the number of cars at Wood Green
allowed the type to be used on route No 39A,
Enfield-Bruce Grove. The former LUT route
No 7 was converted on 15 November 1936.
Prior to this conversion, the ex-LUT cars had
been moved from Hanwell to Hampstead,
where plough carrying gear was fitted. After
the modification, the cars returned to Hanwell
until route No 7 was converted, after which
they were all transferred to Telford Avenue.

6 March 1938 was to witness the conversion
of route No 21, when Finchley lost its remaining
'Felthams' and the first ex-MET cars were sent
south of the river. The final conversion affect-
ing the 'Felthams' at this time occurred on
8 May 1938 when routes No 29 and 39A were
converted. The remaining 'Felthams' were
transferred to Telford Avenue. The last to arrive
was No 2077, which was delayed due to acci-

Ex-LUT 'Feltham' No 2141 is seen on 30 December 1950
operating on the peak hours only service from Savoy Street
to Tooting. This was one of the routes to be converted
during Stage 2 of 'Operation Tramaway' on 6/7 January
1951. No 2141 was to last slightly longer, being one of the
final batch of 'Felthams' withdrawn in April the same year.
It later became Leeds No 570 and survived until 1957. It
was scrapped at Low Fields Road Yard in October the same
year. V. C. Jones/IAL

dent damage being repaired. The transfer was achieved by running the cars, unusually, through the Kingsway Subway.

The 'Felthams' were now destined for a decade of life on unfamiliar metals. Based at Telford Avenue, or Brixton Hill, the cars operated normally on routes serving Tooting, Streatham, Purley and Brixton. Minor modifications were undertaken (such as the replacement of route stencils with destination blinds and the fitting of quick release air brakes). The onset of World War 2 and the Blitz were to have serious consequences on public transport in London and the trams were not to escape unscathed. Two 'Felthams' (No 2113 on 26 October 1940 and No 2109 on 24 August 1944) were to be destroyed as a result of enemy action. Other cars were damaged, but the general malaise was lack of maintenance at a time when the pressures were inevitably elsewhere.

After the cessation of hostilities, the greatest need for London Transport was to restore services to prewar standards. Although the abandonment of the tramway system was still the long term aim, the pressures of postwar austerity meant that, for the meantime, the trams would have to soldier on. Between 1945 and 1950 eight of the class were withdrawn. The first to succumb was No 2122, which was scrapped at Brixton depot in July 1947 after sustaining accident damage in a collision at Clapham during 1946. In September 1949, No 2099 was sent to Leeds on trial; it entered passenger service in December of that year, retaining its London number until it was renumbered 501 in August 1950. Prior to entering service in Leeds it was repainted in an-LT style red and cream livery and saw its twin trolleybooms and plough carrier replaced by a bow collector. Six (Nos 2067/91/130/163/165/167) were scrapped at Purley depot in December 1949. Following No 2099's successful operation in Leeds, it was decided that the northern city would acquire the entire fleet of surviving 'Felthams' at a price of £500 each.

The fate of the remaining London trams was sealed when, on 5 July 1950, Lord Latham, Chairman of the London Transport Executive, announced a £10 million scheme for the conversion of London's remaining trams — 'Operation Tramaway'.

At the announcement of 'Operation Tramaway' in 1950 there remained a total of 90 'Felthams' still in service. The 'Felthams', no doubt as a result of the deal with Leeds, were to be amongst the first casualties of the programme. Indeed six cars of the class (Nos 2066/69/70/77/82/97) were withdrawn in August before Stage 1 of the conversion programme took place. The first stage — which affected routes in the Clapham and Wandsworth area — saw the demise of 23 of the type (Nos 2071-76/78/80/81/83-88/93/96/100/105/108/115/116/118). After withdrawal the 'Felthams' were prepared for their journey to Leeds.

Between Stages 1 and 2, three more (Nos 2144/62/64) were withdrawn as a result of a fire at Brixton depot on 18 November 1950. The first two were destroyed, whilst the third, No 2164, was repaired and despatched to Leeds. In order to maintain the order from Leeds, the unique car, No 1, was sent north, becoming No 301 in the Leeds fleet.

Stage 2 was to witness the demise of a further nineteen of the remaining cars (Nos 2068/89/90/92/94/95/98/101-104/106/107/110-112/114/117/119). This stage, on 6/7 January 1951, saw the withdrawal of trams in the Balham and Tooting area. The cars were again despatched to Leeds. Two additional cars,

Nos 2079 and 2123, were also withdrawn at this time, but were subsequently reinstated. Prior to Stage 3 No 2139 was damaged in an accident and withdrawn. Repaired, the car was sent north. Stage 3, on 7/8 April 1951, was to see the final demise of the 'Felthams' in London. A total of 40 were withdrawn with the closure of routes to Purley, Thornton Heath and Croydon. The cars withdrawn were mainly ex-LUT vehicles, although the last ex-MET car, No 2079, also succumbed at this stage. The last car to head northwards was No 2158, which departed from Charlton on 3 October 1951.

Heading northwards, No 501, as it had become, emerged partially repainted on 3 August 1950 having had side destination panels fitted. The first of the newly acquired cars, No 2097, arrived in the city on the 12th of the same month. It emerged on 12 September 1950 as No 502 in an experimental livery of red and green. It was not to retain the somewhat garish livery for long! No 502 entered service with another two on 22 September 1950.

On arrival in Leeds the cars underwent considerable work at Kirkstall. As the trams arrived more quickly than it was possible to process them, the new arrivals were stored at Torre Road to await the call. The trucks were completely stripped down and any worn parts were replaced. Whilst the bodies were found to be generally sound, improved destination displays were fitted. The front exit was not restored and the cars emerged in the new red livery adopted by Leeds to replace the earlier blue colours (before the final version was adopted, a number of 'Felthams' appeared in a variety of liveries, although red always predominated). In addition to the other work, the 'Felthams' were now fitted with a bow collector in place of their traditional trolley poles.

By late 1950 a total of 32 'Felthams' had arrived in Leeds and the first livery variants were beginning to appear. Nos 506 and 508, for example, appeared with an additional cream band above the cab window, whilst No 509 sported cream window frames. By mid-1951 a total of 66 'Felthams' had headed north. The initial cars were based at Torre Road depot, but Nos 504 and 505 were sent to Swinegate for crew training on the Kirkstall, Dewsbury Road-

Compton Road/Gipton services. New arrivals were, however, still being stored at Torre Road to await their turn in Kirkstall Works. The last of the 90 'Felthams' acquired, No 2158, arrived in Leeds on 6 October 1951. In Leeds the ex-MET cars were classified 'UCC/1' and the ex-LUT vehicles 'UCC/2'.

So far all the 'Felthams' to enter service had been the ex-MET cars; this was inevitable given that the ex-LUT cars lasted longer in London. But the first of the ex-LUT cars to enter service in Leeds, No 551 (ex-No 2139), did so on 26 October 1951. By mid-1952 a total of 68 were operational; Nos 501-20 were based at Swinegate (for routes to Kirkstall, Roundhay, Meanwood, Dewsbury Road, Compton Road, Hunslet, Belle Isle and Hyde Park) with the remainder at Torre Road (for Whingate, New Inn, Cross Gates, Halton and Temple Newsam). No other depots ever had an allocation of the class. The 'Felthams' were not permitted to operate to Beeston as they lacked mechanical track brakes. It was not until July 1957, when the cars were fitted with modified sanding gear, that the type started to operate over the Middleton circle.

In January 1951 No 517 appeared with an experimental pantograph. It was followed in March by three further cars, Nos 528-30; all four, however, had bow collectors fitted by June. It was reported in 1952 that one of the 'Felthams', No 519, was in Kirkstall Works for a trial conversion in to a single-deck vehicle. The scheme was destined not to be progressed and there were now straws in the wind that indicated that the long-term future of the trams in Leeds was in doubt.

One of these indicators was that the remaining 22 cars, which had yet to enter service, saw no work undertaken on them for more than two years. Moreover, one of the cars that had entered service, No 507, was involved in an accident at Roundhay Park with No 92 (which was scrapped) on 4 September 1952. The 'Feltham' was put into store and was destined never to be repaired. It was eventually scrapped in August 1955. Far more serious for the trams was the adoption of a tram conversion policy by the local Labour Party in March 1953 and, when the Labour Party achieved power in May of the same year, the fate of the trams was decided. The new abandonment programme was adopted in June 1953.

Between 1954 and 1956 much of the reserved track on the York Road routes was relaid. Due to the high axle weight of the 'Felthams' the condition of the track had deteriorated. The weakened track severely affected the cars' bolsters and axle springs.

No 524 waits outside Kirkstall Road depot on 26 April 1951. Amongst modifications undertaken in Leeds were the fitting of Fischer bow collectors and side destination panels — both of which are visible in this photograph.

Although conversion was now Leeds' avowed policy — and indeed the first conversions had already taken place — work restarted on the remaining 'Felthams' in early late 1954. The first to appear were Nos 563/70/80; No 563 had its normal controllers replaced with interlocking Metro-Vick MV0K9B controllers — probably from withdrawn 'Pivotal' cars — in order to reduce the type's tendency to slip when starting on greasy track. Further cars appeared over the next 18 months — Nos 564-69/73/74/82/85/87/89. The last car to enter service, No 582, appeared on 31 July 1956; this was the last tram to be commissioned in Leeds. By this date Torre Road depot had closed, and all the 'Felthams' were concentrated at Swinegate and could be seen on all the surviving routes with the exception of the Middleton service. On 21 July 1956 No 585 was to operate the last public service when route No 16 to New Inn was converted to bus operation.

That the commissioning of No 582 was to be the end of the programme was confirmed by the disposal of the seven cars which never entered service. The first to go was No 576 in July 1956, which was scrapped at Kirkstall Works. It was followed in August by No 577 and by No 578 in September. These three cars had never been renumbered in Leeds and retained their London livery to the end. Seven cars were to be dismantled at Low Fields Road Yard in November and December 1956. These included the last four cars that had not entered service (Nos 571/72/75/84) which, like the earlier three, had retained their London livery and the first three (Nos 552/55/79) from the operational fleet, which had been withdrawn in July of that year.

The three operational cars withdrawn in July 1956 were all ex-LUT GEC-equipped cars and, like the 'Horsfields', the problem in obtaining spares for the GEC cars was one factor in their early demise. In order to obviate the problem, Leeds re-equipped a number of the GEC cars with OK9B controllers. The cars so treated were many of the ex-LUT cars that entered service in 1955-56 (Nos 563/68/73/74/82/85/87).

These withdrawals left a total of over 70 available, all of which were now painted in the Leeds livery. Although the Leeds system was rapidly contracting — nine routes had been withdrawn between October 1953 and July 1956 — the 'Felthams' were relatively

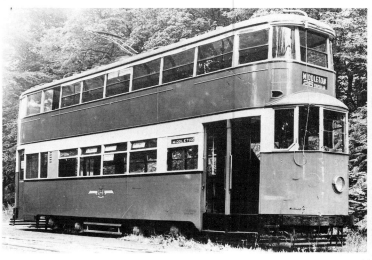

The first of the LPTB 'Felthams' to reach Leeds, No 2099, initially ran in the Yorkshire city wearing its original London livery and bearing its original LPTB fleet number. Following the acquisition of the remaining 'Feltham' cars No 2099 was eventually numbered 501 although it continued to run in its London livery until a repaint was due. Although the car shows Middleton as a destination, 'Felthams' only operated over that route from July 1957 when modified sanding gear was fitted. *Real Photographs/IAL*

unscathed as the older and non-standard classes gradually succumbed. The last of the ex-Hull cars was withdrawn, for example, in 1956 as was the last 'Pivotal'. In its last three years, the Leeds system was effectively to be operated solely by 'Horsfields' and 'Felthams' so that even in 1957 repainting of the cars at Kirkstall continued.

September 1957 saw the conversion of the routes to Moortown and Dewsbury Road, and this led to the withdrawal of 19 'Felthams' — 12 BTH fitted and seven GEC — and these cars were all scrapped by December of that year at

Two of the earlier 'Felthams' in Leeds — Nos 505 (ex-LPTB No 2069) and 515 (ex-LPTB No 2093) — pass in the early 1950s. Note the variation in livery; during this period there were numerous experiments designed to identify the most suitable version of the new crimson and cream fleet livery. *Ian Allan Library*

The York Road routes, with much of their track on central reservations, were destined to be the last routes converted in Leeds. 'Feltham' No 566 heads towards the city on route No 12 *en route* to Middleton, whilst 'Middleton Bogie' No 268 heads eastbound towards Cross Gates. No 268 was one of the last two of this attractive design to survive, being scrapped in October 1957. The 'Feltham' was to last until April 1959. *D. Trevor Rowe*

Low Fields Road. Just prior to the September conversions, the first renumberings occurred when Nos 505/20 and 511/19 swopped numbers. Other renumberings also occurred right through until February 1959. The end of 1957 also saw the end of the track connection to the works at Kirkstall; in future all overhauls would be undertaken at Swinegate, with the trucks transferred by road to Kirkstall for attention. No 568 and 'Horsfield' No 194 were the first cars to be overhauled and repainted at Swinegate. Other cars repainted by early 1958 included Nos 529/74/82; not all was positive, however, as No 513 was placed in store following an electrical fire in December 1957 and was destined not to operate again.

1958 was a relatively quiet year for the system; there were no routes converted and there were no 'Feltham' withdrawals. This meant that the final year of the Leeds system opened with eight routes remaining operational and some 50 'Felthams' in service. These comprised 31 ex-MET cars and 19 ex-LUT. Of the ex-LUT fleet all those converted to OK9B controllers remained operational. On 28 March 1959 the first conversions for almost 18 months occurred when three services — Nos 3 (Briggate-Moortown), 12 (City-Middleton via Moor Road) and 26 (City-Middleton via Belle Isle) — were abandoned. No 512 was the last passenger car to operate on the No 26 circular. As a result of the 28 March closures six cars (Nos 522/54 [ex-517]/61 [ex-587]/64 [ex-557]/81/88) were sold to Joseph Standish Ltd of Hunslet for scrap and a further five (Nos 513/63/65 [ex-524]/66/67) to Johnson of Churwell.

The next route to be converted was No 25 to Hunslet on 18 April 1959. A further 20 cars — Nos 502/09/10/11 (ex-519)/18/21/24 (ex-565)/35/36/49/56/57 (ex-564)/68/69/73/74/82/85/87 (ex-561)/89 — were sold to George Cohen Ltd for scrap in June and July 1959, and were dismantled in a yard at Holbeck. This left only 19 'Felthams' in service, of which only one — No 517 (formerly No 554) — was ex-LUT. Routine maintenance work continued to be carried out; No 526, for example, had a truck overhaul in August 1959 and this later was a factor in its preservation.

The final closures occurred on 7 November 1959 when the remaining four routes, along

No 546 is seen in City Square on route No 15 to Whingate in c1955. No 546, originally London Transport No 2101, was to be one of 17 'Felthams' to survive until the final closure of the Leeds system in November 1959. After closure the car was scrapped in Swinegate depot. *T. Darnbrough*

WHINGATE
15

546

HAMMONDS Guards Ale

TAILOR

York Road, to Harehills Lane (No 17), Cross Gates (No 18), Halton (No 20) and Temple Newsam (No 22) were converted. Although the 'Horsfields' — as traditional Leeds trams — operated the bulk of the 'last' services, No 531 did have the honour of being the last service car to Temple Newsam at 4.2pm; No 512 was the last 'Feltham' in public service. Of the 19 extant cars at the closure, 13 saw service on the final day — Nos 501/05 (ex-520)/12/14/23/25/26/28 (ex-539)/29/31/32/38/42 — whilst the remaining six — Nos 504/06/15/17 (ex-554)/534/46 — were stored.

After closure all the remaining cars, with the exception of three preserved, were sold to J. W. Hinchliffe Ltd and scrapped in Swinegate depot; the last to be scrapped disappearing in February 1960. Of the three production cars preserved, No 501 (ex-LPTB No 2099) passed to the Museum of British Transport at Clapham, where it arrived on 3 December 1959. After closure of the Clapham Museum, the car passed to London Transport and, as MET No 355, now forms an integral part of the London Transport Museum collection at Covent Garden. A second ex-MET car, No 526 (ex-LPTB No 2085), was purchased by the Seashore Museum in the United States and left Leeds for Liverpool on 9 March 1960 for shipment to the New World. It reached its new home on 28 March 1960. The third car, and the only ex-LUT 'Feltham' to survive, No 517 (ex-554) passed to the Middleton Railway Preservation Society and was stored eventually at the railway's Parkside site. Unfortunately, after vandalism, the car was burned for scrap on 20 April 1968.

The MET 'Felthams'

MET No	LPTB No	Withdrawn	Leeds No	To service	Withdrawn
319	2066	9/50	506	11/50	11/59
321	2067	4/49	-	-	-
322	2068	1/51	539	1951	11/59
323	2069	9/50	505	10/50	10/57
324	2070	9/50	507	11/50	8/55
325	2071	9/50	530	1951	10/57
326	2072	9/50	521	9/51	7/59
327	2073	9/50	508	12/50	8/57
328	2074	9/50	510	1951	7/59
329	2075	9/50	527	1951	10/57
330	2167	4/49	-	-	-
331	2168	8/36*	-	-	-
332	2076	9/50	524	1951	4/59
333	2077	8/50	503	10/50	8/57

334	2078	9/50	509	12/50	7/59
335	2079	4/51	550	9/51	10/57
336	2080	9/50	516	1951	9/57
337	2081	9/50	520	1951	2/60
338	2082	8/50	504	10/50	2/60
339	2083	9/50	525	1951	12/59
340	2084	9/50	519	1951	7/59
341	2085	9/50	526	1951	11/59**
342	2086	9/50	528	1951	9/57
343	2087	9/50	518	1951	7/59
344	2088	9/50	512	1951	11/59
345	2089	1/51	537	1951	8/57
346	2090	1/51	544	1951	9/57
347	2091	3/49	-	-	-
348	2092	1/51	533	1951	8/57
349	2093	9/50	515	1951	11/59
350	2094	1/51	538	1951	11/59
351	2095	1/51	543	1951	8/57
352	2096	9/50	523	9/51	11/59
353	2097	8/50	502	10/50	7/59
354	2098	1/51	542	1951	11/59
355	2099	9/49	501	12/49	11/59**
356	2100	9/50	513	1951	4/59
357	2101	1/51	546	1951	11/59
358	2102	1/51	534	1951	11/59
359	2103	1/51	548	1951	8/57
360	2104	1/51	532	1951	11/59
361	2105	9/50	511	1951	10/57
362	2106	1/51	531	1951	11/59
363	2107	1/51	541	1951	9/57
364	2108	9/50	522	1951	5/59
365	2109	8/44	-	-	-
366	2110	1/51	536	1951	7/59
367	2111	1/51	545	1951	10/57
368	2112	1/51	547	1951	10/57
369	2113	10/40	-	-	-
370	2114	1/51	540	1951	10/57
371	2115	9/50	514	1951	11/59
372	2116	9/50	529	1951	11/59
373	2117	1/51	549	1951	7/59
374	2118	9/50	517	1951	5/59
375	2119	1/51	535	1951	7/59

Notes:
All entered service with MET from February 1931 onwards and the entire batch was operational by the end of that year.
* Sold to Sunderland (No 100) and eventually preserved.
** Preserved cars; No 341 in USA; No 355 at London Transport Museum.
The following cars were renumbered:
       505 to 520 August 1957
       511 to 519 August 1957
       517 to 554 February 1959
       519 to 511 August 1957
       520 to 505 August 1957
       524 to 565 November 1958
       527 to 528 July 1957 and to 539 August 1957
       528 to 527 July 1957
       539 to 528 August 1957

The LUT 'Felthams'

LUT No	LPTB No	Withdrawn	Leeds No	To service	Withdrawn
351	2120	4/51	557	1951	4/59
352	2121	4/51	558	1951	10/57
353	2122	4/51	573	4/56	8/59
354	2123	4/51	564	3/55	7/59
355	2124	4/51	-	-	-
356	2125	4/51	561	1952	7/59
357	2126	4/51	565	2/55	7/59
358	2127	4/51	568	4/56	8/59
359	2128	4/51	572	-	11/56
360	2129	4/51	574	6/56	7/59
361	2130	c1948	-	-	-
362	2131	4/51	555	1951	12/56
363	2132	4/51	569	7/55	8/59
364	2133	4/51	582	7/56	8/59
365	2134	4/51	566	3/55	4/59
366	2135	4/51	584	-	11/56
367	2136	4/51	567	4/55	4/59
368	2137	4/51	559	1951	11/57
369	2138	4/51	554	1951	11/59
370	2139	2/51	551	10/51	9/57
371	2140	4/51	563	2/55	4/59
372	2141	4/51	570	10/55	10/57
373	2142	4/51	578	-	9/56
374	2143	4/51	581	1952	4/59
375	2144	10/50	-	-	-
376	2145	4/51	577	-	8/56
377	2146	4/51	579	1952	12/56
378	2147	4/51	587	6/55	5/59
379	2148	4/51	560	1951	9/57
380	2149	4/51	580	2/55	7/57
381	2150	4/51	553	1951	11/57
382	2151	4/51	576	-	7/56
383	2152	4/51	556	1951	7/59
384	2153	4/51	588	1952	4/59
385	2154	4/51	589	3/55	7/59
386	2155	4/51	571	-	11/56
387	2156	4/51	575	-	11/56
388	2157	4/51	586	1952	10/57
389	2158	4/51	590	1952	10/57
390	2159	4/51	585	6/56	7/59
391	2160	4/51	583	1952	9/57
392	2161	4/51	562	1952	10/57
393	2162	10/50	-	-	-
394	2163	c1948	-	-	-
395	2164	10/50	552	1951	12/56
396	2165	c1948	-	-	-

Notes:
The following cars were renumbered:
        554 to 517 in February 1959
        557 to 564 in February 1959
        561 to 587 in February 1959
        564 to 557 in February 1959
        565 to 524 in November 1958
        587 to 561 in February 1959

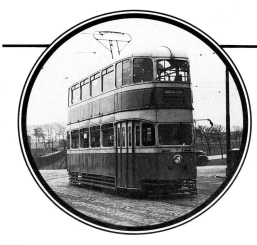

11.
The
'Cunarders'

Of the four Scottish tramway systems to survive after 1945, Glasgow was, by far, the largest. With over 1,100 trams in service Glasgow came historically second only to London in terms of British operators; indeed, such had been the decline in London prior to 1939 that Glasgow had become the single largest operator. However, much of the fleet was formed by the huge class of 'Standard' cars constructed over a 25-year period from 1899 onwards and even by the late 1930s the increasing age of the 'Standards' was giving serious cause for concern.

As part of a policy of tramway investment in the 1930s 152 streamline 'Coronation' bogie cars were constructed in the Corporation's workshops at Coplawhill. These cars, which were fitted with EMB Lightweight bogies, were built between 1936 and 1941 and were part of a much larger programme that envisaged a total of 600 modern cars being constructed. In the event, the outbreak of war led to the curtailment of the programme. Thus, many of the 'Standards', which should have been withdrawn in the 1930s, were left to soldier on for almost another 20 years.

Unlike many other major operators which had had no definite abandonment programme before 1939 (such as Liverpool), Glasgow continued to develop its tramway system in the late 1940s. Although there were minor abandonments, such as the Duntocher route in 1949

(with the consequent demise of the cut-down ex-Paisley trams), and the conversion of two routes to trolleybus operation in the same year, these closures were partially offset by the opening of two extensions — Carnwadric in 1948 and Blairdardie in 1949.

Initial thoughts for further new trams were formulated in late 1945. The intention was to produce a tram, similar in design to the prewar model, but simpler and with a larger seating capacity. In November 1945 Eric Fitzpayne, the General Manager, advocated the acquisition of 100 trams and in March 1946 the tenders were received. Formal approval was given on 2 May 1946. Although the overall price for bogie cars was significantly higher than that for four-wheelers, it was agreed that bogie cars would be ordered. The electrical equipment was to be

The 1,000-strong fleet of Glasgow 'Standards' represented the second largest single class of British tramcar following the LCC 'E/1s'. Built over a 25-year period and much modified, by the early 1950s the type was increasingly perceived as being a liability and one of the pressures for the construction of the 'Cunarders' was the desire to replace many of the older 'Standards'. 'Standard' No 658 is seen at Auchenshuggle on 23 March 1949.

The failure to complete the full 600 cars in the prewar 'Coronation' programme meant that many of the existing 'Standards' were required to continue in operation. The 'Cunarders' or 'Coronation' Mark IIs, were a more utilitarian version of the prewar cars. The last new cars to be constructed for Glasgow, Nos 1393-98, reverted to the prewar form. 'Coronation' No 1283 is seen at Millerston on 23 March 1949.

supplied by Metropolitan-Vickers with the bogies supplied by Maley & Taunton. The bodies were to be built partially of resin-bonded Canadian birch plywood (for the side panels) and aluminium and sheet steel for the dashes. Construction started in June 1947 and No 1293 was completed by December 1948.

The 'Cunarders', or 'Coronation Mark 2s', differed significantly from the older design. They were six inches longer, at 34ft 6in, than the prewar cars and could seat (in Nos 1293-1348) a total of 70 passengers — 40 in the upper and 30 in the lower saloons. Later cars, from No 1349 onwards had the seating capacity reduced to 66 (40 in the upper, 26 in the lower), which still compared favourably with the 65 seats of the 'Coronations'. The trucks were M&T type 596s, with a wheelbase of 5ft 6in (as opposed to the EMB Lightweight, with a wheelbase of 4ft 6in, of the 'Coronations') and four Metro-Vick MV109AR motors, rated at 35hp. The 'Coronations' had four BTH109AR motors, also rated at

35hp. The 'Cunarders', at 14ft 11in, were also about nine inches lower than the earlier cars. The design of the bodies owed a great deal to the unique single-ended car, No 1005, which had been completed earlier. A number of the modifications, such as the single-piece windscreens, were later adopted when the prewar 'Coronations' underwent overhaul.

The first 'Cunarder', No 1293, entered service in a non-streamlined livery and a similar style was adopted for all deliveries up to No 1300. From Nos 1301 to 1339 a semi-streamlined livery was used, with the intermediate colour band between the decks bisecting the destination blinds. On all cars, except No 1303, this intermediate band was green; the exception had a red band. Finally, the remaining cars, Nos 1340-92, received the full streamlined livery; all the earlier cars were eventually treated similarly. The last car to retain a non-standard livery was No 1300, which appeared in 1954 after a period of storage at Newlands depot due to a fault.

Unfortunately, the introduction of the cars was not without problems. Poor running of the bogies over sleeper track led to representatives of Maley & Taunton visiting Glasgow to investigate, with the result that dampers were introduced. This modification improved the ride. There were also problems with the brake cylinders on the earlier cars. These had been con-

A number of non-standard trams were constructed by Glasgow during the 1940s. These included the unique single-ended car No 1005, which is seen here at Newlands depot on 19 June 1949 in its blue livery. The design of the 'Cunarders' owed much to the design of this car, for example in the adoption of the single-piece windscreen and the use of similar trucks.

structed from malleable steel in order to save weight, but proved unsatisfactory in operation.

During 1949 the construction of 'Cunarders' suffered serious delays as a result of the workload at Coplawhill and, in order to accelerate the programme, both Pickerings (who had built the new streamlined cars for Aberdeen) and Hurst Nelson, were approached to see if either company was interested in constructing around 50 of the cars. Although potentially the biggest postwar contract for new trams, Hurst Nelson, one of the country's best-known and long-established tramcar manufacturers, declined to tender, although their more recent competitor did. In the event, a deputation from Coplawhill led to an increased labour force in the works and an increased rate of production as all the work was retained in Glasgow's own works. The episode makes an interesting parallel with the 1930s, when one of the factors behind the decision to maintain and modernise the tramway system and build the 'Coronations' was the desire to maintain, rather than reduce, the workforce at Coplawhill.

Although a suggestion was made, in April 1949, that 10 of the cars be built as single-deckers — to facilitate safer and quicker loading and unloading, possibly over route 12 (Mount Florida - Paisley Road Toll) — all 100 cars were completed as planned. The last car, No 1392, entered service on 13 February 1952.

All new cars were allocated to Newlands depot on entry into service. Between 1954 and 1957, Newlands depot retained Nos 1293-336, whilst the remainder were transferred to Govan. In early 1955 some of the Govan-based cars were transferred to Possil depot — the first modern cars to be allocated there — although they continued to operate on routes Nos 4, 22, 27 and 32. In mid-1958 21 of the type (Nos 1372-92) were transferred from Govan to Dalmarnock depots, for use on services Nos 9, 10, 17, 18 and 26; Govan depot closed as an operational depot in November 1958. This brought the type on to routes using Argyle Street for the first time. Following the conversion of route No 8 (Millerston-Rouken Glen) on 15 March 1959, some 'Cunarders' were transferred from Newlands depot to Partick. Thus, gradually, as the Glasgow network contracted to the most modern trams, including the 'Cunarders' migrated from their traditional routes and depots to the remaining services.

When photographed at Millerston on 23 March 1949 the prototype Mark II 'Coronation' or 'Cunarder' No 1293 had only been in service some three months. It had taken almost 18 months to complete, which was symptomatic of the somewhat long drawn out production life of the 100 cars of the type. The first eight cars, Nos 1293-300, were delivered in a completely non-streamlined livery, but were eventually to be repainted. It was discovered that the iron protective rail beneath the side panels interfered with crane lifting and jacking.

By January 1960 the once great Glasgow network had declined to some 13 services and a fleet of some 400 cars. Of the various classes operational, only the 'Cunarders' remained wholly intact; the first of the 'Coronations' had been withdrawn the previous year, whilst the ex-Liverpool 'Green Goddesses' had been slowly withdrawn from 1957 onwards. The situation was, however, soon to change, with the demise of No 1390 on 21 January following accident damage. Two more, Nos 1295 and 1350, were destined to be withdrawn in April 1960 but the remainder of the class — with the exception of No 1296 withdrawn in August and No 1343 in December — was to survive into 1961. Six routes, however, were converted to bus operation during the year and significant numbers of the remaining 'Standards' as well as other 'Green Goddesses' and 'Coronations' were withdrawn.

'Cunarder' No 1382 is seen in the company of one of its elder brethren — 'Standard' No 104. No 1382 has had its upper deck half-drop window replaced with a hinged flap to improve access to the bow rope. This car was to survive until the end of the system, unlike No 104, which was to be scrapped in October 1958. *Real Photographs/IAL*

The fate of 25 'Cunarders' (Nos 1316/23-26/31/33-35/37/44-47/53/54/65/68-70/76/86-88/91) as well as numerous other cars was determined on 22 March 1961 when the important depot at Dalmarnock caught fire. The demise of so many modern cars led to a temporary reprieve for many of the remaining 'Standards' and certain of the cars designated for preservation were also pressed back into service. The severe shortage of stock that the fire could have caused was, however, reduced

'Cunarder' No 1338 entered service on 14 June 1950 and was to survive until 27 August 1962. It is seen here on the service to Mosspark, via Pollokshields, which was converted to bus operation on 4 June 1960. *W. J. Haynes*

by the conversion earlier in the month of route No 16 (Scotstoun-Keppochhill Road) to bus operation. With the withdrawal of three other cars in early 1961 (Nos 1298/301/81), a total of 67 'Cunarders' remained in service out of a fleet of some 200 cars.

The temporary shortage of cars resulting from the Dalmarnock fire ceased on 3 June 1961 when routes Nos 18 and 18A (Springburn-Burnside/Shawfield) were converted. Although there were to be two further conversions later in 1961 — when on 21 October route No 29 (Tollcross-Maryhill) was converted and route No 26 cut back from Farme Cross to Dalmarnock — only two more 'Cunarders' were to be withdrawn that year — No 1389 in June and No 1342 in November.

Thus a total of 65 were to survive into the last year of Glasgow's tramway history, operating over the three remaining routes. The total fleet had been reduced to around 185 in number. January and February were to see four further casualties (Nos 1329/64/66/84). The next closure occurred on 10 March when route No 15 (Anderston Cross-Baillieston) was converted to bus operation. Partick depot closed at this stage, with all remaining cars allocated to the remains of Dalmarnock depot for the two remaining services.

Between March 1962 and the end of July a further six of the class were withdrawn — Nos 1300/02/03/15/40/55 — leaving over half

the class in service at the start of the system's last full month. The penultimate route to close — No 26 Clydebank-Dalmarnock — was converted to bus operation on 2 June 1962. The last car to operate on the service to Dalmarnock was No 1318, which carried a card proclaiming 'This is the last 26 tram'. It left the terminus at 12.6am to head for Dalmarnock depot.

This closure left only one service — route No 9 Dalmuir West-Auchenshuggle — in operation and withdrawals were now coming more rapidly. In August, 16 of the class were withdrawn for scrap (Nos 1296/99/304/05/08/10/27/28/36/38/41/59/73/75/77/78) and from June onwards the bodies of the scrapped cars were sold to Wilmots of Partick and transported to the scrapyard by lorry. Coplawhill continued to dispose of the trucks. By early September, and the final closure of the system, 38 of the class remained in stock and many were to be involved in the system's final rites.

Inevitably, the closure of the system was marked by a number of specials. On 26 August the Scottish Tramway Museum Society hired No 1321, whilst on 1 September there were no less than three simultaneous tours, which used

'Cunarders': No 1389 was hired by the Omnibus Society and No 1360 (along with No 1222) by the Tramway & Light Railway Society. 1 September was to see the final regular services over the one remaining route. The last service car from Auchenshuggle to Dalmuir was No 1383 arriving at 11.26pm, which departed for Yoker. It was followed to Yoker by No 1313, which became the last service car and which carried a notice announcing 'The End of the Greatest British Tramway'. No 1313 arrived back at Dalmarnock depot finally at 12.55am.

Over the next three days, 2-4 September, special services operated between Anderston Cross and Auchenshuggle. The first of these days was operated entirely by 'Coronation' cars, 'Cunarder' No 1308 appearing on the Monday, whilst two, Nos 1339 and 1360, operated on the Tuesday. The honour of being the final car to carry fare-paying passengers on 4 September passed, however, to 'Coronation' No 1174. The closure procession on 4 September included no less than eight 'Cunarders' — Nos 1297/352 (which were reserved for the staff)/63 (reserved for the STMS)/67/79/82/85 (which had had a complete repaint for the

event)/92. During the procession, No 1392's lifeguard came adrift whilst the car was traversing London Road. Prompt action by a member of the LRTL ensured that only a 10min delay ensued. The closure procession finally reached Coplawhill at 7.30pm.

Even this was, however, not to be the end of the system. On 6 September 'Coronation' No 1282 was used for an official farewell in Clydebank, whilst at closure 62 trams remained in Dalmarnock depot. These were moved to Coplawhill over five days from 11-15 September, with No 1165 being the last to make the trip. No 1392, preserved by the Museum of British Transport at Clapham as the last all-new double-deck tramcar built in Britain, left Glasgow on a Pickfords lorry heading south on 11 September.

The scrapping of the remaining cars proceeded rapidly, so that by 16 November only three 'Cunarders' remained intact in Barrland Street yard. Of these No 1297 was destined for preservation at Crich, whilst the remaining two, Nos 1352 and 1367, were both scrapped by 22 December 1962.

Thus the story of the single largest class of postwar trams built in Britain came to an end. Two of the cars were to survive, No 1297 at Crich and No 1392, initially at Clapham and then returned north on the closure of the museum — along with a bogie from No 1377, which is displayed in the Glasgow Museum of Transport.

'Cunarder' No 1321 heads east along Argyle Street under the Central station bridge. Entering service in February 1950, this was one of the batch (Nos 1301-39) that entered service with the semi-streamlined green band. By the date of this photograph the car had received a fully swept down green band. *W. J. Haynes*

12

The Sheffield 'Roberts'

The steel city of Sheffield had one of the most compact and well-run of all British tramway operators. Although constrained by the gradients and sharp curvature on certain routes to operating only four-wheel cars, the city's Transport Department had ensured that its fleet of blue-and-white cars had been largely modernised during the late 1920s and 1930s. Over 270 trams had been built both by the Corporation and by outside suppliers between 1927 and 1939. In addition, 14 cars had been rebuilt during the war to replace cars destroyed during the Blitz.

However, the need to strengthen the fleet during the war had led to the purchase of 14 second-hand trams from Newcastle and 10, which had to be regauged, from Bradford. The Newcastle cars dated from 1905-7 and the ex-Bradford ones from 1919-1921. In addition, there remained some 150 trams dating from before 1925; the oldest of these being delivered in 1907.

From the investment both in vehicles and routes undertaken in Sheffield during the 1930s, it is clear that the Transport Department felt that the tram had a long term future in the city and authorisation was given for the construction of a new four-wheel car in the Corporation's works at Queens Road. The new car, No 501, made its first trial run on 11 July 1946. It was 32ft 6in long and provided accommodation for 36 seated passengers in the upper saloon and 26 in the lower. The car was fitted with a 9ft wheelbase Maley & Taunton hornless truck; this truck was unique in Sheffield at the time. It was both longer than any other Sheffield truck and its wheels — at 2ft 3in — were of smaller diameter. The car was constructed using a steel underframe on which a composite body was built. The car lacked traditional bulkheads — the first Sheffield tram so

built — and was provided with fluorescent lighting in both saloons. This latter feature was also only to be found on No 501 of Sheffield's fleet. Two Metro-Vick 65hp motors provided the power and control was obtained through BTH controllers. After successfully passing through its trial programme, No 501 officially entered service on 12 August 1946.

The completion of No 501 was to mark the end of an era in Sheffield. It was to be the last new car constructed by the Corporation. All new trams were, in the future, to be supplied by outside contractors. Inevitably No 501 was to prove popular for hire on enthusiasts' tours, such as that on 22 September 1946 — its first — and that organised by the LRTL on 22 May 1949.

By this date it was clear that No 501 was soon to be joined by a batch of 35 new cars, vehicles which would allow for the withdrawal of many of the ex-Newcastle and ex-Bradford cars. Authorisation had been gained from the Ministry of Transport in early 1948 by the Corporation to borrow £200,000 to fund the acquisition of new trams. The successful bidder for the contract was Charles Roberts & Co of Horbury, near Wakefield.

Charles Roberts was one of relatively few entrants into the tram building industry in the postwar era; apart from the batch of cars for Sheffield the company is perhaps best-known for the building of the 25 'Coronation' single-deck cars for Blackpool.

Delivery of the cars was slow, however, and the first, No 502, did not enter service until 15 May 1950. Although outwardly similar to the original car, there were a number of significant alterations. The most fundamental was that the new cars had all-metal bodies, rather than the composite body of No 501. Conventional, rather than fluorescent, lighting was fitted and

Above:
**Between 1919 and 1927 Sheffield received 150 traditional
double-deck trams supplied by either Cravens or Brush.
These were the last cars supplied to Sheffield with rocker
panels. No 452, of the Cravens-built batch of 1926-27, is
seen at Crookes on 1 January 1954.**

Below:
**Between 1927 and 1935 Sheffield had constructed, either in
its own workshops or by outside builders, some 200 flush
panel 'Standard' cars to replace older cars in the fleet.
No 73 is seen *en route* to Weedon Street during September
1949. Like all of Sheffield's fleet these cars were four-
wheelers.**

Following on from the 'Standard' cars, Sheffield constructed 67 domed-roof cars, such as No 256 seen here at Crookes on 22 May 1949, between 1936 and 1939. A further 12 of the type were constructed during World War 2 to replace cars destroyed by enemy action. These were the last new trams acquired before No 501.

Below
No 501 is seen on a Southern Counties Touring Society tour on 28 August 1949 alongside an earlier generation of Sheffield tram — No 94 — which was one of 70 cars built at Queens Road Works and delivered between 1930 and 1933. *V. C. Jones/IAL*

the external side-lights were slightly lower than on No 501, being located in the lowest cream panel rather than the narrow blue band beneath the lower saloon windows. At 32ft 7in, the production cars were one inch longer than No 501, but retained the 9ft wheelbase Maley & Taunton truck. Motors were of the Metro-Vick MV101-DR3 type, rated at 65hp each, and the controllers were BTH B510s, which incorporated the air brake operating valve chamber. The cars emerged in the standard Sheffield livery of blue and cream, with maroon underframe. On 13 August 1950 No 503 became the first 'Roberts' car to operate a tour and by December 1950 Nos 502-510 were in service. They were usually operated on the Middlewood/Ecclesall, Intake/Walkley and Prince of Wales Road circular routes. Delivery of the cars increased over the next 18 months. Nos 511-513 were delivered in December 1950, Nos 514-531/33/34 arrived during 1951, leaving only Nos 532/35/36 for delivery in 1952. The last of the batch, No 536, entered service on 11 April 1952.

In August 1950 the then six postwar trams were allocated to Holme Lane (Nos 501/03/05) and Shoreham Street (Nos 502/04/06). Of the cars then awaited, five (Nos 516-20) were scheduled for allocation to Tinsley, four (Nos 508/10/12/14) to Shoreham Street, five (Nos 507/09/11/13/15) to Holme Lane and one (No 521) to Tenter Street).

Top left:
The interior of 'Jubilee' No 501 pictured on 28 August 1949. This was the first Sheffield car to be delivered without interior bulkheads and was unique in the Sheffield fleet in being fitted with fluorescent lighting. A total of 10 fluorescent strips were provided for the upper deck.
V. C. Jones/IAL

Bottom left:
The interior of the upper deck of one of the Roberts -built cars. The seats, which were provided for 36 passengers, were manufactured by Siddall & Hilton Ltd with red leather upholstery. On the lower deck, seating was in moquette with green leather trim. *Ian Allan Library*

However, by 1952 the promise for the future indicated by the purchase of the 35 new trams was shown to be illusory. On 4 April 1950 the Transport Committee presented a report to the City Council, which advocated the conversion of the city's tram system to bus operation over a 13-year period from January 1952 to mid-1965. Despite opposition from the Sheffield Tramways Development Association, conversion became the official policy and, with the abandonment of the Malin Bridge and Fulwood routes on 5 January 1952, the inexorable process of conversion started.

Inevitably it was to be the older cars that were to succumb first during the abandonment programme. The ex-Newcastle and ex-Bradford cars were all withdrawn by the end of 1952 and the last of the UEC cars of 1907 disappeared in 1954. Inroads were soon made into the fleet of 'Rocker Panel' cars and by 1957/58 the first of the modern prewar cars had succumbed. It was clear that the rate of conversion made the 15-year deadline generous; by 1959 the tram fleet, which had once stood at almost 500 in number, had been reduced to 100 — including the 36 postwar cars. The entire fleet was now allocated to Tenter Street depot. The 'Roberts' cars were still less than a decade old, and there were rumours in 1958 — which came to nought — that the cars were to be sold abroad.

1960 was, in the event, to be the last year of Sheffield's system. The first of the 'Roberts' cars to be withdrawn was No 520, which was taken out of service on 3 April 1960 after the conversion of the Sheffield Lane Top-Woodseats/Meadowhead service. The next withdrawals were Nos 511, 512, 525 and 533, which all required new tyres and which were, there-

The unpainted bodyshell of one of the 'Roberts' cars prior to delivery to Sheffield. The photograph shows clearly the all-metal body of the type.
Ian Allan Library

No 502 was the first of the 'Roberts' cars to be delivered and its arrival was recorded in the contemporary transport press. Pictured when brand-new, No 502 illustrates well the azure blue and cream livery applied at Sheffield's Queens Road Works. *Ian Allan Library*

Left:
'Roberts' car No 507 is seen at the terminus at Middlewood prior to departure to Ecclesall. On delivery in 1950 the car was initially allocated to Holme Lane depot. The Middlewood-Ecclesall service was one of the early casualties of the Sheffield abandonment programme, being converted to bus operation on 27 March 1954. *Real Photographs/IAL*

fore, withdrawn on 10 August 1960. Like all withdrawn cars, these were taken to Tinsley shed (on 12 and 13 August 1960) to await the one-way trip to the scrapyard. At about the same time Nos 510 and 513 were despatched to Queens Road for repainting in a commemorative livery.

A further three cars, Nos 505, 531 and 532, were to succumb before the end of September since repairs were no longer being undertaken. Two more, Nos 508 and 524, were sent to Tinsley on 7 October having developed faults. Of the remaining 'Roberts' cars 14 (Nos 501/02/06/09/14/15-17/19/22/26/28/35/36) were in regular service on the last day — 8 October 1960. These, and the other surviving trams, were gradually replaced by buses during the course of the final afternoon. Each tram's final duty ensured that it reached Tinsley — there were to be no ghostly movements of trams from depot to depot after final closure in

In May 1953 No 533 awaits departure on a Woodseats, via Queens Road, service. With the introduction of advertising on the side panels, the Corporation monogram, which had graced the cars on introduction, was discarded. *Ian Allan Library*

Sheffield unlike other systems. No 502 was the last service car to Beauchief, whilst No 517 fulfilled a similar role at Vulcan Road. Appropriately, No 536 was the last service car to leave Tenter Street depot. Fifteen trams, including 12 'Roberts' cars, formed the final procession, which departed from Tenter Street depot shortly after 6pm. Nos 503 and 504 carried members of the Council and their guests, as did the specially repainted duo of Nos 510 and 513, whilst the remaining eight cars carried members of the public. Shortly after 8pm, No 504 became the last car to reach Tinsley.

There only remained the final rites to be undertaken. Conveniently, the scrapyard of

Thos. W. Ward was situated adjacent to the Tinsley shed and between October and 21 December an almost daily movement saw a tram make its progress across the road. Again, appropriately, the last car to make the journey was No 536, which was transferred on 21 December.

Fortunately, however, two of the 'Roberts' cars were to escape into preservation. No 510 departed for Crich and arrived at its new home on 29 October 1960. It remains at the National Tramway Museum and retains the specially painted panels that it acquired in 1960. The second surviving 'Roberts' car, No 513, has had a more itinerant life since withdrawal. It travelled to the Middleton Railway, near Leeds, on 3 December 1960 where it was stored along with a number of other trams. Fortunately, however, it was to escape the fate of the majority of the cars 'preserved' at Middleton, being transferred to the old goods shed at Cullingworth (near Bradford) in 1963. From there it

With ex-Great Central 'D11' No 62670 *Marne* shunting above, No 520 heads under the Wicker Arch *en route* towards Sheffield Lane Top. *Kenneth Field*

spent a short period in the open at Oxenhope on the Keighley & Worth Valley Railway before being stored on behalf of the Castle Museum (York) at Fulford. It arrived at the North of England Museum, Beamish, in 1977 and has subsequently been fully restored. The restoration required the loss of the decorated panels and these have subsequently passed to the National Tramway Museum. During 1985 No 513 was one of the guest trams in Blackpool to mark the centenary of the town's tramway system.

Top:
Looking slightly the worse for wear, No 523 was however to survive until the end of the system. It was one of 12 members of the class to be involved in the closure procession, and carried members of the public. After withdrawal, the car made its one-way journey to Ward's scrapyard on 7 December 1960. *Real Photographs/IAL*

Above:
Pictured on 8 October 1960 — the last day of tramway operation in Sheffield — No 515 picks up passengers prior to departing for Millhouses. A second 'Roberts' car can be seen following it in the distance. *D. Trevor Rowe*

13.
The Aberdeen 'Streamliners'

Apart from the isolated Cruden Bay line of the Great North of Scotland Railway, Aberdeen could lay claim to being the northernmost electric tramway in the British Isles. It was also, for many years, regarded as being one of the most forward-thinking and progressive operators. Whilst it was a relatively small system, and such systems had been prominent amongst the closures of the 1930s, Aberdeen had strengthened its fleet during that decade through the judicious acquisition of second-hand trams. However, such a policy was not a means of ensuring the system's long term survival.

Thus, in 1940, the Corporation obtained four streamlined cars built by English Electric. These four cars were numbered 138-141. The order, which had been placed by the Corporation prior to the outbreak of the War, was split between bogie and four-wheel cars in order to evaluate both types prior to the placing of substantial orders for fleet replacement.

Nos 138 and 139 were bogie cars. They were fitted with EMB bogies and with four English Electric Type 327 34hp motors. The cars could accommodate 44 passengers in the upper saloon and 32 in the lower, although the total seating capacity on both cars was reduced to 74 in 1952.

The second pair, Nos 140 and 141, were four-wheel cars. They were fitted with EMB swing axle trucks and with two English Electric Type 305 57hp motors. The trucks included EMB's patented built-in air brakes. The seating capacity of the four-wheel cars was 64.

The English Electric bodies on both types were similar, although the bogie cars had centre entrances/exits with separate cab doors for the drivers. The four-wheel cars had a conventional rear-end platform arrangement, with the driver's cab reached through a door off the platform. When delivered, the cars were painted in a reversed livery of predominantly cream with green bands. However, a more normal fleet livery of green, with cream bands was adopted later, although all the streamlined cars were to have, throughout their career, a greater amount of cream than the older type cars.

With the cessation of hostilities in 1945 thoughts could once again turn to the development of the tramway system. Aberdeen in the late 1940s was one of the few operators that could be reported on positively at LRTL conferences and, whilst the half-built route to Sea Beach was not completed despite hopes that it would be, at least the city had no active policy aiming at conversion. The problem of fleet replacement remained significant and, as a result, Aberdeen was one of four operators to acquire the 'Pilcher' cars made surplus by the conversion of Manchester's network.

There still remained a need, however, to replace some of the older cars in the fleet and authorisation was given to the acquisition of 20 new streamlined cars. Although the batch was built by R. Y. Pickering of Wishaw, the company was acting as a sub-contractor to English Electric and the cars owed much to the design of the earlier English Electric cars. The underframe was produced from rolled steel sections and the composite body was constructed using steel panels over an oak frame. Window mullions were constructed out of aluminium. Four English Electric EE327 motors, rated at 34hp each, were fitted as were EMB 5ft 0in wheelbase lightweight bogies. The overall length of the cars was 38ft 0in and they could seat a total of 76 (32 in the lower saloon and 44 in the upper) on transverse seating. As with the earlier bogie cars, the batch was provided with centre-entrance bodies with separate cabs for the drivers. Fischer bow collectors, standard in Aberdeen, were also fitted.

Above:
The Aberdeen fleet was, until the delivery of the prototype streamlined cars, highly traditional — indeed it continued to operate open-balcony cars into the early 1950s. Here two of Aberdeen's pre-streamlined cars are seen on Castle Street on 24 January 1949. No 2 was one of a batch of 18 cars bought second-hand from Nottingham in 1936 and was originally new in 1926. Five years older, No 89 was constructed in the Corporation's Works.

Below:
Prior to the delivery of the first of the streamlined cars in 1940 the last wholly new trams to be constructed for Aberdeen were traditional four-wheelers built by Brush in 1929. No 128, of the batch of 12, is seen at Queen's Cross on 24 January 1949.

One of the two bogie streamlined cars delivered in 1940, No 138, is seen when new. The first four streamlined cars were delivered in a reversed livery of largely cream with green bands. The offside cab door for the driver is clearly visible. *Ian Allan Library*

The first of the batch, No 19, entered service on 27 January 1949 on the Hazlehead route, and by the following month a total of four had been delivered. The remainder of the batch was received and in service by August of the same year. The cars were operated over the whole of the Aberdeen system, with the exception of the Woodside route, since the length of the cars meant that it was not possible to accommodate two in the St Nicholas Street terminal loop. The delivery of the new cars allowed for the withdrawal of some of the ex-Nottingham cars, but the high hopes for the new cars were somewhat dimmed by the high operating costs incurred.

The lack of air-operated doors meant that the trams had to be crewed by three staff (a driver and two conductors) and the expense could not be justified throughout the year. As a result it was normal for many of the cars to be withdrawn during winter months and operated during the remainder of the year through the employment of students as ancillary conductors on the Bridge of Don-Bridge of Dee and Hazlehead-Sea Beach routes.

Clearly, such an arrangement was wasteful of expensive equipment and from relatively early in the type's career efforts were made to ameliorate the situation. In 1952 the lower deck seating was altered from transverse to longitudinal (reducing the seating capacity from 32 to 30 in the lower saloon), which allowed for an increase in the number of standing passengers from 10 to 20. In late 1953 authorisation was given for the testing of air-operated centre doors and No 30 was so fitted during mid-1954. The cost of the conversion was estimated at £200. The doors were now controlled by the driver, through the use of two buttons, and this allowed for the tram to be crewed by a single conductor.

The success of the test conversion of No 30 led to the authorisation for the modification of a further five cars, including No 24, at a price of around £2,000. It was estimated that the alteration would save an average of £1,050 per annum.

No doubt, had the Aberdeen system had a long term future by 1955 then the remainder of the cars would have had a similar modification, but in February 1955 it was announced that the Corporation was to undertake the conversion of the tram system to bus operation. Two closures had preceded the official announcement — Mannofield in March 1951 and the Rosemount Circle in October 1954 — and this left effectively four routes in operation. November 1955 saw the conversion of the Woodside route, to

Above:
The driver's cab on wartime streamlined car No 138. Clearly visible is the offside cab door. *Ian Allan Library*

Right:
The second of the bogie streamlined cars, No 139, is seen at the Bridge of Don terminus in 1947. At this date the car retained its original seating arrangement but, in 1952, the capacity was to be reduced by two.

Below right:
No 141 was the second of the four-wheel streamlined cars and was delivered in 1940. The differences between this and the earlier bogie cars are very apparent — eg the traditional platform arrangement and the lack of a separate cab door for the driver. The car is seen at the Hazlehead terminus on 10 June 1948. Although sister car No 140 was to be withdrawn in 1956, No 141 lasted until closure in 1958. In the last few years, the folding doors on these two cars were replaced by roller shutters.

be followed in October 1956 by that to Hazlehead and in November 1956 by Woodend. The route to Sea Beach, the penultimate to close, was finally withdrawn in March 1957.

The first of the streamlined cars to be withdrawn was No 140, which succumbed in 1956, but the rest of the cars survived until 1958 and the final closure. During a snowstorm on 19 January 1958 all the bogie streamlined cars were temporarily withdrawn and replaced by the surviving older four-wheel cars. By May 1958 only a total of 11 trams remained available for service; these were Nos 19-24/26/29/32/36/37 — the majority of the remaining cars had been cannibalised for spare parts.

No 20 was destined to be the last car in ordinary passenger service. It was scheduled to depart Bridge of Don at 6.52pm and Castle Street at 7.3pm. One of the postwar batch, No 36, was to be the official last tram on 3 May 1958 when the final route, Bridge of Don-Bridge of Dee, was converted to bus operation; Nos 32/33/37 also featured in the closure pro-cession. A total of 41 cars remained in stock at closure, including the surviving 23 streamlined cars.

Although the streamlined cars were offered to Blackpool — who expressed a certain amount of interest in them — the relatively small seating capacity (74 as opposed to 94 on one of the Blackpool 'Balloons') along with the possibility that a number of routes might be converted, meant that Blackpool did not pursue its interest. As a result all the surviving trams were sold to W. T. Bird of Stratford-upon-Avon, and were scrapped at Sea Beach. Unfortunately, none of the streamlined cars survived into preservation.

No 33 awaits departure from the Castle Street terminus of route No 4 to Hazlehead. The extension of the route to Hazlehead beyond Woodend was converted to bus operation on 7 October 1956 with the rest of the route following on 17 November the same year. *Real Photographs/IAL*

Above:
Seen when almost new on 1 April 1950, at the Bridge of Dee terminus, No 36 awaits departure for the northern terminus of Bridge of Don. It makes an interesting comparison with the open-balcony car behind. The size of the streamlined cars, and the lack of air-operated doors, meant that crews of three were required to operate them.

Below:
No 36 is seen again, this time at the Hazlehead terminus on 28 May 1955. This route was to be converted to bus operation on 7 October 1956. No 36 was to survive until the end of Aberdeen's system, when it was to be the official last car.

Appendix 1:
Principal Dimensions of the Types covered

Type	Numbers	Built	Builder	Trucks	Length	Height	Width	Seating capacity	Stairs	Withdrawn
Aberdeen	19-38	1949	Pickering	EMB Bogies	38ft 0in	15ft 2in	7ft 2in	44/32	Straight	1958
Belfast	392-441	1935-6	EE/Service	M&T	32ft 0in	15ft 9in	7ft 9in	40/24	Normal 90°	1950-4
Blackpool										
Standard'	See text	1922-9	BCT/HN	Preston bogies	33ft 10in	16ft 3in	7ft 2in	46/32	Direct 90°	1940-66
'Streamlined'	284-303	1937	Brush	EMB bogies	42ft 3in	15ft 9in	7ft 6in	48	Single-deck	1962 onwards (12 in service)
Dundee	19-28	1930	Brush	EMB	33ft 0in	15ft 6in	7ft 3in	34/28	Normal 180°	1956
Glasgow	1293-392	1948-52	GCT	M&T	34ft 6in	15ft 3in	7ft 4in	40/26	Normal 180°	1961-2
Huddersfield	137-44	1931-2	EE	M&T	29ft 0in	15ft 3in	7ft 0in	38/20	Normal 180°	1940 (Note 1)
Leeds	155-254	1931	Brush	Peckham P35	31ft 5in	15ft 6in	7ft 5in	37/23	Normal 90°	1956-9
Liverpool:										
Bogie	151-88, 868-992	LCT	1936-7	EMB/M&T	36ft 9in	15ft 0in	7ft 4in	44/34	Straight (with 90° turn)	1942-56 (Note 2)
Four-wheel	201-300	1937-42	LCT	EMB	33ft 10in	15ft 5in	7ft 4in	40/30	Straight (with 90° turn)	1942-57
London										
'Feltham'	2066-165	1931	UCC	EE/EMB	40ft 10in	15ft 11in	7ft 2in	42/22	Straight (with 90° turn)	1940-52 (Note 3)
'HR/2'	101-59	1930-1	HN	EMB	33ft 10in	15ft 7in	7ft 1in	46/28	Direct 90°	1940-52
'HR/2'	1854-903	1930	EE	EMB	33ft 10in	15ft 7in	7ft 1in	46/28	Direct 90°	1939-52 (Note 4)
Manchester	See table	1930-2	MCTD	Peckham P35	32ft 6in	15ft 8in	7ft 3in	40/22	Direct 180°	1946-48 (Note 5)
Sheffield	502-36	1950-2	Roberts	M&T Hornless	32ft 7in	15ft 9in	7ft 0in	36/26	Normal 180°	1960

All figures are rounded to the nearest inch. The dimensions and data given are designed to cover the bulk of the type. Any variations and alterations can be found in the relevant chapters.

Notes:

1. The eight Huddersfield cars were sold to Sunderland (Nos 29-36) and were finally withdrawn in 1953-4.
2. The 'Green Goddesses'. Forty-six were sold to Glasgow in 1953-4; see table.
3. The 'Felthams' were originally built for London United and Metropolitan Electric Tramways. The cars passed to the LPTB in 1933. Apart from two cars destroyed during World War 2 the remainder survived until 1945. The bulk of the class were sold to Leeds in 1949-51, although not all entered service. The last were withdrawn by Leeds in 1959.
4. Three of the ex-LCC 'HR/2s' (Nos 1881/83/86) were sold to Leeds (Nos 277-79) and were finally withdrawn in 1957.
5. The 'Pilcher' or 'Pullman' cars were sold to Leeds (7), Sunderland (6), Edinburgh (11) and Aberdeen (14). The last (in Aberdeen) were withdrawn in 1956.

Appendix 2:
List of Preserved Examples of Trams Covered in This Book:

Type	Fleet number	Location
Aberdeen	None preserved	
Belfast	None preserved	
Blackpool		
'Marton Box'	31	Beamish
'Standard'	40	Crich
	48	Oregon USA
	49	Crich
	144	Seashore USA
	147	Ohio USA
	159	Carlton Colville
'Streamlined'	11	Carlton Colville
	226	California USA
	228	California USA
	298	Undergoing restoration for Crich
Dundee	None preserved	
Glasgow	1297	Crich
	1392	Glasgow
Huddersfield	None preserved	
Leeds	180	Crich
Liverpool		
'Green Goddess'	869	Crich
'Baby Grand'	245	Liverpool
	293	Seashore USA
London		
'HR/2'	1858	Carlton Colville
'Feltham'	2085	Seashore USA
	2099	London Transport Museum
Manchester	None preserved	
Sheffield	510	Crich
	513	Beamish

Left:
Unfortunately, only one of the 'Horsfields' survives in preservation: No 180 at the National Tramway Museum. Another two were to escape the scrapyard, only to be eventually dismantled at the Middleton Railway. No 180 is seen in its home town on 24 October 1948. The car is painted in the blue livery, but with the large fleet number.

Right:
Blackpool 'Standard' No 49 is one of two of the type to be preserved at the National Tramway Museum and one of six of the type preserved in total. A seventh was also to pass to Crich for use as spares, but was finally dismantled.